HOW TO SELL IN THE NEW ECONOMY

THE SALES PROFESSIONAL'S GUIDE TO THRIVING WHERE OTHERS FAIL

ERIC LOFHOLM

ROCK WARRIOR PUBLISHING
LAS VEGAS, NEVADA

Visit our Web site at **www.EricLofholm.com** for more information on Eric Lofholm.

Library of Congress Control Number: 2010925382

ISBN: 978-0-9844097-0-9

Published in the United States of America by
Rock Warrior Publishing
6285 East Spring Street, Suite 387
Long Beach, Ca 90808-4000

ATTENTION BUSINESSES AND PROFESSIONAL ORGANIZATIONS: Quantity discounts are available on bulk purchases of this book for educational, gift purposes, promotional, or as premiums for increasing magazine subscriptions or renewals. Special books or book excerpts can be created to fit specific needs. Contact the Director of Special Projects at dsp@RockWarriorLLC.com.
You can also call (800) 551-4376.

Table of Contents

Page
_____

The Sales Mountain

1

Selling can be incredibly profitable. Fast cars, a big house and a comfortable retirement are yours, once you know how to sell. It can also be extremely fun when you have the knowledge necessary to be a top sales person, and you know how to apply it.

The Sales Profession is one of the few professions in the world where someone who does not have a college degree and may not have even finished high school, can still be very successful. In fact, you can easily earn a living on par with, and in many cases, in excess of, a medical doctor.

Yet, despite the potential, you may struggle with selling. That is understandable and it is really not your fault, because the rules have changed. The way in which Americans buy has dramatically changed due to the Great Recession. We are now living in a new economy. Through this new economy, many sales professionals just like you have seen their incomes crumble to rock bottom levels.

However, there is hope. Right now there are sales professionals that are earning more money than at any other time in their careers. You can be among them. The astute sales professional is taking full advantage of this current market turmoil to bring in more leads, more clients, and converting that to more income for them and their families.

Before you can take the principles and practices that these top sales professionals are implementing in their businesses, a proper understanding of the Sales Mountain is in order.

Sales Mountain? You may be thinking, "What the heck is a Sales Mountain?" So let us give an illustration and then talk about the Sales Mountain.

The Sales Mountain is a process similar to having a meal at a restaurant like the Olive Garden. If you go to the Olive Garden with your spouse and friends, the first question they usually ask is, "How many in your party?" You reply, "There are four of us." They proceed to provide you with a coaster that will light up when your table is ready. You and your friends then have a seat in the waiting area and when the coaster lights up, you go up to the hostess and they seat all of you.

The first question the waiter usually asks is, "Would you like to start off with a beverage? Or would you like an appetizer?" Then it moves onto, "Would you like soup or salad? What would you like for an entrée?" Then they bring you the food; they make sure the food is cooked properly by asking how you like your meal. Later, after you have finished your entre, they offer you coffee and dessert, and then they bring you the bill. At the Olive Garden they always give you what with the bill?

If you answered the green Andes mints, you are right!

That is the process at the Olive Garden. Now, instead of the above process, can you imagine that when you first sit down, the waiter says "Would you like to start off with a slice of cheesecake?" Of course your answer is "No." The reason why your answer is no, is that question at that time is *not the correct sales process.*

The way I teach the sales process is through strategies and techniques I call the Sales Mountain.

Part of selling is education. So if you sell a product or service that is new to the person that you are sharing it with, like reverse mortgages for example, there is an educational component to your Sales Mountain. If you are selling a reverse mortgage, it is most likely the first time the homeowner has ever done a reverse mortgage. So you have to educate them on all the details of a reverse mortgage, then they can understand it. I am sure you have found in your sales career that people will seldom buy what they do not understand.

One way to educate people is to use scripts to connect the known to the unknown. This is where the Sales Mountain begins, so let us examine it in more detail.

Step 1) Lead Generation
Step 2) Appointment Setting
Step 3) Trust and Rapport
Step 4) Identify Customer Needs
Step 5) Share the Benefits
Step 6) Close
Step 7) Objection Handling
Step 8) Follow Up

There are two wild cards that also need to be correctly played:

1. **Qualifying** your lead
2. Obtaining **Referrals** from your new client

The big idea to get here is there is a process to how you set yourself up for sales success. Most people prior to meeting me have never given much thought to what the process is. They go and they wing their presentation. Always remember when you wing it you get inconsistent results; preparation, preparation, preparation. It is your preparation that will set the foundation to your success when you follow the Sales Mountain steps one through eight.

Every time you learn new ideas, you become more effective at the next presentation you deliver. You are going to have your new skill set for the rest of your life. It is going to help you make tens of thousands if not hundreds of thousands, maybe even millions, in increased commissions. What I am sharing with you is not theory. It is not what I think you should do. It is what I and other successful sales professionals do on a daily basis. I follow my Sales Mountain and in following it, I have fun. Selling becomes easy and effortless, and I consistently close my deals.

The Sales Mountain

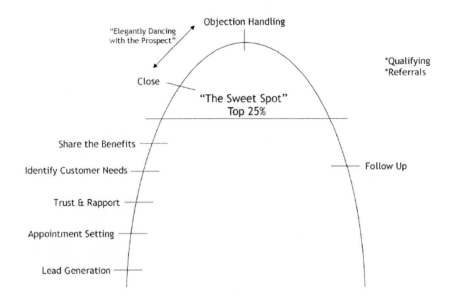

One aspect of the Sales Mountain is a concept called stage selling. In stage selling you sell the prospect to the next step. On your very next presentation, before you go into the presentation, you will want to think about it and think about what is your desired outcome for that presentation? What is it that you want to accomplish? What is the result that you are looking for? Are you trying to book an appointment, are you looking to get a referral, are you looking to close the sale, are you looking to book a follow up appointment, are you looking to create a joint venture or strategic alliance? You go in with a predetermined outcome. Here is a golden nugget for you; go into every presentation that you deliver with a predetermined outcome of what it is that you want to accomplish. Because you really do get what you focus on.

I had a conversation recently with a client and they are in a place in their life right now where their cash is really tight. They need to make more money immediately. In that conversation I said "Look, you need to have ninety five percent of your business energy going into what is going to create cash right now." This is a time when they have really got to be on their A game. It is the same thing with you. Unless you are just flooded with business right now, you have got to be on your A game as well. A lot of companies are going out of business, but the companies that are making it are making it big because they are capitalizing on opportunities, while the competition is not.

I was at Chili's restaurant the other day and they were pretty busy. I took my daughter Sara, who is four, and my wife. They were really busy because their competitors have been going out of business. Dr. Moine, a leader in the sales psychology field, would have called this a thinning of the herd. So this is a time to be on your A game.

This is also a time to be in your massive action mode!

Let me give you an example of a day with massive action. Yesterday my day started off at 6:30am. I got in my car and drove down to have a meeting in Marin County with my master mind partner, who is Brian Klemmer, and also met with the person who runs Brian's company, a gentleman by the name of Bob. I had a 10:00 AM conference call where I was selling to a group of about one hundred people. I delivered that call, and then went back and continued my mastermind session. When I finished with that session, Loral Langemeier and I did a webinar promoting our upcoming seminar in San Diego. We chose to do a webinar that people could watch so they could see and not just hear the value of what we are going to be teaching that day. Then I went back and worked on my masterminding some more. After that I held another webinar. Then I drove to Burlingame and spoke to a group of professional organizers, after which I drove home.

When I got home I finished up the day with some e-mail. Not every day is like that. But one of the ways that I am getting ahead in this economy is I am in a place of massive action. I am not telling you to have your life out of balance, I am just simply stating this is not a time to slow down; this is a time to speed up. This is a time to sharpen the saw, work on yours skills and collaborate.

Today I had two meetings with potential joint venture partners. One of them has a four thousand person database, the other has a twelve thousand person database and these are great business people for me to work with. They both told me that they want to collaborate with others. I share that with you because people are interested in collaboration right now. If you are not currently collaborating with others I want you to be open to adding that to your baseline.

Baseline Strategy:
Whatever you are currently doing; this is your baseline. Keep doing what you are doing and then add one or more new ideas or activities to your baseline. This will increase your results.

One gentleman I talked with recently (a very successful business person) said to me, "Eric, I will sum up my year in one sentence. This is the year of collaboration."

Are you optimizing your joint ventures? If you are not, I encourage you to do so. If you have not done joint ventures, this is something you want to be working towards.

Joint venturing starts with making a list of people that you would like to partner with. When I say partner, it is simply looking for ways that you can add value to each other. As an example, I talked to a group today that has this four thousand person database and I said, "Why don't you sponsor my seminar? You do not have to pay me anything, just promote my seminar to your four thousand person database and then I will make you a sponsor." They loved the idea. That is an easy example of a joint venture.

This step in the Sales Mountain is setting an appointment.

Your only goal here is to set an appointment. That is it.

So let me explain what I mean by an appointment, because it is a broader definition than what you are probably thinking. An appointment means that you get your prospect in front of your product or service. That could be a one-on-one, face to face appointment. It could be a one-on-one appointment over the phone. It could be a group presentation delivered on a webinar. It could be a group presentation on a conference call. It could be a front of the room presentation to a group of people. It could be getting somebody to go to your website, so they can see the offer where they can make a buying decision. It could be you sending out a sales letter that explains your offer to the point where the prospect can make a buying decision. So that is what I mean by an appointment.

After you set the appointment, now you are on the live presentation with the prospect and the first step is trust and rapport. One of the things you will notice, when you listen to how I sell (you can all listen, if you are on a conference call where I am offering one of my programs) is I follow a script. That script keeps me on track to follow the Sales Mountain.

I have a structure for my presentation, and the first thing that I do on a conference call is I build trust and rapport. I did it on a call today:

> *"Hi this is Eric, who just joined the call?" And then the person says their name. I say, "Hi welcome, thanks for joining us." I greet people when they come on to the call. The reason why I do that is that is a rapport building step. Then the next thing that I do, on a conference call where I am selling, is I acknowledge people for being on the call. I tell them that they have greatness inside of them. I believe in them. What that is doing is that is building rapport. It is not in a phony way. It is absolutely in a sincere way because I think it is a huge deal when people take time out of their lives to listen to a conference call that will make them better at selling.*

From an influence standpoint, the reason why you want to do this is to align with the prospect.

Rapport reduces resistance.

The next step in the Sales Mountain is to identify customer needs. The easiest way to persuade or influence someone is to find out what they want and give it to them.

Think now, about the presentations you have been giving recently. How effective have you been at identifying the true needs of your prospects? Have you been taking the time to ask questions to find out what is most important to them?

One of the mistakes a lot of salespeople make is they go straight for features and benefits and there is a place for that; but before we go to features and benefits, we want to find out what is *important* to this person. The way we find out what is important is by asking questions.

A good way to start is by making a list of probing questions that you can ask your prospects prior to delivering your next presentation. Now, part of the power of this process is the order in which you proceed.

Remember at the Olive Garden, where the waiter hypothetically asked *"Would you like to start off with a slice of cheesecake?"* It was a reasonable question but not as the opening question to ask when you sit down at your table. So the sequence that you ask is very important.

It is called a reasonable request at a reasonable time.

It is a reasonable request to say "Will you marry me?" but not on a first date. Think of the process of dating. First you might say, "Would you like to go out to coffee?" And then you go out on a date; then you become girlfriend and boyfriend; and then you become exclusive; and then you get engaged; and then you get married. And that is the process.

This is the process of Identifying Customer Needs – reasonable request, reasonable time.

The next step in the Sales Mountain is to share the benefits. At the end of the day, people buy benefits. There are tangible benefits, like safety, decreases in turnover, and the warranty on the program. Then there are the intangible benefits, like peace of mind, increased confidence, prestige, etc.

Then there is the benefit of taking action. The benefits enjoyed by your potential client in moving forward today. And remember, there is also the consequence of not taking action. What they will miss out on by not taking action.

Finally, there is the benefit of the benefit. Oftentimes this is the real reason why people buy. The reason why people buy from me is not really because I am effective at teaching sales skills and it is not actually because they want to learn sales skills. The reason people become a client of mine is they understand the benefits which enhanced sales skills will produce for them.

And once people learn these skills, they have them for the rest of their life.

Imagine you are making an extra five thousand dollars a month, what would be different for you in your life?

Imagine that right now. Would you be able to once and for all completely get out of debt? This is one of the gifts that I create for my clients.

What is your dream car? Would you drive your dream car? Would you move into a new home? One of my clients, Arvee Robinson, had been renting for eight years and she wanted to become a homeowner again. She is in her fifties now. And, last year with my help, she became a homeowner for the first time in eight years.

Do you want to invest for retirement? Are you scared of running out of money in retirement? Do you want to become the top producer in your company? Do you want to win the cruise that your company has offered to their top salespeople?

See, these are the reasons why people ask for my assistance. I get them connected to the benefit of the benefit and I want to encourage you to do the same with your clients. Now, one of the great things that you can do that will make you more powerful and effective on every presentation that you give for the rest of your life – is to tell success stories.

Nothing motivates like success stories. *Nothing sells like success.*

This is important, nothing sells like success. I want to share with you a couple of stories of clients that I have worked with.

The first one is a gentleman named Joey Aszterbaum. When I met Joey he was an average loan officer. The best month that he had ever had produced about ten thousand dollars, which was pretty good, but it was not consistent.

So, I went out to his office and I did a free sales training at his company, Patrion Mortgage, and at the end of that free training, I offered my protégé program. This is an opportunity for people to mentor with me.

Joey saw a value in working with me, so he signed up for the program. I started teaching him all these ways to be more successful in his selling. Six months later, he earned over thirty thousand dollars in a single month. Last year, Joey took four weeks of vacation because he was doing so well. He was able to take four weeks of vacation which is more vacation than he has taken in the previous five years combined.

With my help, he went from an average loan officer to a superstar.

Most realize that last year the loan industry was down overall. I was working with Joey at the beginning of last year. In the protégé program I help my members create a one-year sales and marketing plan. Joey created this plan and he sent it to me in the beginning of the year and his goal was to do forty-eight loans in the course of the year. I told Joey "you are capable of so much more" and I encouraged him to increase his goal to seventy-two.

Just last year, in that "down year" – true story – while in my mentoring program, Joey Asterbaum did sixty-seven loans!

Let me share with you another success story. I met Wendy Phaneuf on a conference call. Wendy is out of Winnipeg, Canada, and her website is www.leadingforloyalty.com.

Wendy got involved with my training a few years ago. She was not sure if she was going to keep her own consulting business or if she was going to shut it down. She was struggling at that point. She was at a crossroads. She was either going to go back and work at a job or she was going to grow her consulting business. Her confidence was down and she was having a tough time.

She was on one of my conference calls and she connected with my message of selling from honesty, integrity, and compassion. She liked the fact that I had real tools to help people and she signed up for my protégé program.

The next year she tripled her business. Last year, she doubled her business again. She had a goal to take off the entire summer, which she had never done before and she was able to do it! She took the entire summer off! Wendy earned the income of her dreams and she changes people's lives all over the world because she is now a global trainer.

And these are just two stories of hundreds that I have had over the years. I have people email me almost daily sharing their success stories.

When you are sharing the benefits with your prospect, remember that nothing sells like success. Tell them stories of success.

We are now on the sweet spot of the Sales Mountain. The close is the natural conclusion to a well delivered sales presentation.

When I close one-on-one, I ask for the order, and then I am silent. I always close that way.

Think about the Girl Scout selling Girl Scout Cookies. You are out in front of the grocery store, you walk up and there is little Julie. She says to you, "Would you like to buy some Girl Scout Cookies?" And after she asks you that, she is silent. Then you say 'yes' 'no' or you give an objection. Does that script work well? Girl Scouts sell five million boxes of Girl Scout Cookies using that script.

Notice they do not say, "Hi, my name's Julie and here's my business card. On my card it says our website, www.girlscoutcookies.com/Julie; do me a favor when you get home tonight. Purchase a box of Girl Scout Cookies. We accept all major credit cards."

Julie does not do that and the reason she does not do that is because that does not work. Selling is about leading. It is about moving people to action.

You ask for the order and you are silent. The prospect is going to say one of three things. They will say 'yes.' They will say 'no.' Or they will give you an objection. In almost every case, they are going to say one of those things. Yes, no or an objection.

If they say 'yes', then you write up the order. If they say 'no', they say 'no'. This then gives you an opportunity to ask a question and lead them to 'yes'. If they give you an objection, then you are going to elegantly dance with the prospect, again, with questions.

A great metaphor for objection handling is that it is like a game of hot potato. I say to the prospect, "how do you feel about moving forward?"

And the prospect says, "I do not have the money."

So, when I say "how do you feel about moving forward", I am silent and I give the prospect the 'hot potato.' They give me the objection and they give me the hot potato back.

Now that I have the hot potato, I give them the hot potato back OR I give them the hot potato back and ask for the order. However, I do not believe in arm-twisting, high-pressure techniques in the close.

I believe in *elegantly dancing* with the prospects.

In a later chapter of this book I am going to zero in on objection handling techniques to aid in the elegant dace.

There are two wild cards in the Sales Mountain; qualifying and referrals. The reason qualifying is a wild card is you do not have to qualify in every case. It depends on what you are selling.

As an example, my Ultimate Selling Power Seminar is a free one day seminar and I do not qualify people for that seminar. Meaning anybody can sign up. You do not have to qualify to come to the program. It is open to the general public. If you said; "Eric, I would like to bring my sixteen year old son to the program." I will say "Great, bring him to the program." So qualifying is a wild card because in some cases you do not qualify, while in other cases you do qualify.

Getting a referral is another wild card because there are multiple places that you can ask for referrals. You can ask for referrals before the person becomes a prospect or before they become a client. You can ask during your initial presentation. You can ask after they become a client. There are multiple places you can ask for referrals so that is why referrals are a wild card.

I want to give you a distinction within the Sales Mountain for those in network marketing and those that are managers that hire commission only sales people. I have something I call the Enrollment Mountain. The Enrollment Mountain is similar to the Sales Mountain; it is just a slightly different language for those primarily involved in network marketing.

The Enrollment Mountain is as follows:

Step 1) lead generation
Step 2) appointment setting
Step 3) trust and rapport
Step 4) identify customer needs
Step 5) share the vision
Step 6) show me the money
Step 7) enroll
Step 8) address concerns

One thing you have to do in a network marketing presentation is get people to imagine how their life would be different if they were making additional income. That is a critical piece in that type of a presentation. Then instead of the word 'close' as used in network marketing, enrollment is used. Finally, instead of handling objections, it is handling concerns and then following up.

For the remainder of this book I am going to drill down on the vital areas of the Sales Mountain, and what to do so that you can be as successful as you choose to be, in our new economy.

Creating A Sales Plan

$$\boxed{2}$$

This is a very, very important subject as it relates to sales and business, and that is creating a sales plan. If you are honest with yourself, you know it is possible to improve in the area of understanding the numbers of your business.

For some of you, this is a brand-new concept. You are out doing what you are doing but you have not ever really taken the time to think about the numbers. No matter if you are just getting started with understanding how the numbers work, or you are a seasoned pro at the numbers, there is room for improvement. My hope for you is that you can take a few ideas from this section and add them to your business baseline. You will find substantial benefits to being stronger in the area of correctly creating your plan for the rest of your career.

For those of you that have teams of people; you are a sales manager, or you are coaching other people, or you are a consultant, or you are in network marketing, keep in mind the concept, train the trainer. What that means is you are going to get ideas for yourself, and then you are going to take those ideas and you are going to teach them to others. You will find that when you teach ideas to others, you get the concept at a deeper level. If you are on a team, you need to make a commitment to teach at least one person one idea that you learn from this section in the next seven days.

You probably have heard this expression, "selling is a numbers game." It is similar to gambling in Las Vegas. The odds of winning are all in the probabilities of the dice, and the probabilities of the cards. I was watching on television last night a recording of the World Series of Poker. One of the great features included in the show is how with every turn of the card, you can see the mathematical statistics for a winning hand. Poker champions understand these numbers.

There was a guy, a young kid in his early 20's, and he was factoring the probabilities in his head. Suddenly he said out loud that his opponent only had one out. Meaning there was only one card left in the deck that the opponent could get that would beat him. He knew that, based on all the cards on the board, his cards, his hand, the opponent's probable hand, the other guy only had one out. I did not know that, because I do not know cards like that. I have never been a poker player. But this kid understood the numbers, and that is one of the things that had him at the final table at the World Series of Poker.

I am going to suggest that it is extremely important for you to understand the numbers in your business. This is one of the primary differences between successful sales people and unsuccessful sales people. The successful people know the numbers for their business. It may take some research on your part. Remember; when we are talking about numbers, there are many different aspects to think about.

Start by considering the following: How many calls does it take to generate a lead? How many calls does it take to book an appointment? What is the percentage of appointments that you set that cancel?

When I worked for Anthony Robbins many years ago, my sales plan was to run 40 appointments a month, and to schedule 20. They provided us telemarketing to supplement the appointments that we personally set. Setting 40 appointments a month means I wanted to run ten a week. There is five business days in a typical work week. That means I wanted to run two appointments a day. So my business plan became run two, set one.

I averaged a thousand dollars in revenue per run appointment. So I knew if I ran 40 appointments I would generate about $40,000 in gross revenue. That allowed me to anticipate what my commission was going to be. I also knew that about two out of every three appointments that set- ran; one out of every three appointments would go pending or cancelled. Having said all that, since today is Thursday, if I was looking at my calendar of appointments for next week I know that I need about 15 appointments in order for 10 to run, because I know that statistically five are going to go pending or cancelled.

It took me six months to learn those numbers, and once I learned them, my business plan simply became run two, set one. It really simplified what I was doing on a daily basis.

The next number to consider is; what is your average revenue per run appointment? It could be your average income, it could be gross sales, it could be gross profit, it is however you measure results. Then look at your drop-out rate. So what is the cancellation percentage? You probably had times when you have made a sale, and then the client ended up cancelling. It is important to factor that in as well.

These numbers are vital to building a business plan. When you build the business plan you need to begin with the end in mind.

How much income do you want to make? Write this number down now.

How much revenue do you generate per run appointment? Write this down now.

When I asked one of my coaching clients these questions her response was "Well, I am not really sure."

You need to know those numbers so that you can determine if your income target is realistic.

I was on a coaching call with this same client again yesterday and she had just gone on an appointment. It took about 40 minutes to go to this appointment, and it ended up not resulting in a sale. I asked her, "What would you like my help with today?"

She responded with, "Time management."

As we got to talking I said, "You really need to run more appointments." My advice to her was, "You need to start delivering your presentation in a webinar in addition to face-to-face. That way you can meet with some prospects on your computer in your office without having to drive there. This will increase your capacity to run appointments."

I still run appointments face to face and I still do front-of-the-room speeches. Yesterday, I had one front-of-the-room speech at the Shriner's Hospital in Sacramento, and then I had two conference calls. If I had three front-of-the-room presentations yesterdays, I would have been exhausted by the end of the day. But it was a pretty easy day. I had one front-of-the-room presentation and two conference calls. The day before, I did two webinars and one conference call. In the last two days, I delivered six presentations, only one of them was face to face.

Consider that in your business. If you could deliver some or many of your presentations or possibly all of your presentations on webinars or over the phone, how many more presentations could you do in a day?

Ben Feldman has been a sales hero of mine for a long time. There is a wonderful book out called *The Feldman Method*. If you can get a copy of that on the Internet for under $40 you should gobble it up. It is out-of-print so it is regularly priced as high as $95 on the Internet. Feldman was the world's greatest life insurance sales person.

In Feldman's book he revealed that his plan was to sell three insurance policies per week. He called that his track to run on. Now when Ben Feldman started off, he was not a very good salesperson. What allowed him to go from a not very good salesperson to the greatest life insurance sales person ever was what he called "the track to run on." He focused on selling three policies a week. What is nice about this is it is a very doable number. He knew how many appointments he needed to set, and how many he needed to run, in order for him to successfully sell three policies. What is interesting is as he became more and more successful, his goal stayed at selling three policies per week. Another interesting thing about Ben Feldman is he was a scriptwriter. He wrote his own scripts, and in the book, there are many of Ben's personal scripts that he used.

Many years ago when I used to work for Dante Perano, I had to keep track of Dante's numbers. Dante would have a close ratio on his front-of-the-room speech. What I would do is a simple head count. He always wanted to know how many people were in the audience, because he knew that he would close about 25% of the head count. So if there were 100 people in the room, he would anticipate selling 25 units at $795, which is around $20,000 in gross revenue. Not a bad 90 minutes.

What is also interesting is one of the things that allowed Dante to be so consistent with his close ratio is his presentation was consistent. In fact, I remember that I would be at the back table with the road crew and I could lip-sync Dante's jokes. I would be lip-syncing his jokes because he would tell the same jokes at the same time. He mastered that presentation. He realized that if he kept changing his sales scripts he would have no way of being able to predict his closing ratio.

A few years ago I was coaching a gal named Mandy Pratt. Mandy was averaging $1,000 in revenue per run sales appointment. Her appointments were telemarketing calls. So every time she would do the full presentation, on average, she would generate $1,000. So sometimes she'd get $5,000 and sometimes she'd get none, but the average was $1,000. When I was coaching her, we started tracking how many presentations she was delivering monthly. She was coming in around 30-35. And I told her, "Mandy, we need to get you running more appointments. You are doing $1,000 in revenue per run appointment."

Last month she ran 33 appointments, and did $33,000 (approximately) in sales. I said to her, "Mandy, imagine if you'd done 60. You would've more than doubled your income because your gross revenue would have doubled." The dirty little secret is that she was on a sliding commission scale, so her income probably would have tripled!

So I started coaching her on her activity. At the end of that month, I said, "I want you to run 60 appointments next month." So the next month she comes in at 35 appointments. I said, "Mandy, I told you 60. Next month, 60." Next month passes and she comes in at 42. I said, "Mandy, 60." The next month - 38. It took her six months to get it and run 60. And once she got her numbers up, her income dramatically increased. And her average revenue per run appointment stayed at that $1,000 in revenue.

See, she needed to know her numbers. Prior to that, she was not tracking them. If she did not track her appointments, we would have no way of knowing her average revenue per run appointment. I would have had no way to know to coach her. Sixty run appointments is three appointments per day on a 20-day business month.

That is a magical number, the number 20, and you can use that when you are determining what your sales numbers are. At my company, my staff has numbers. They are clear on what the expectation is for the appointments they set and the appointments that they run.

If your average revenue per run appointment is $500 and your goal is $10,000 for the month, you know you need to run 20 appointments. Now here is the thing, even if your numbers are unknown, you can make an educated guess, and still create a sales plan. The way I approach a month is I look at the month, I look at the results that I want to accomplish, and then I break it down in to appointments run.

There are three key systems that I teach. Lead generation, appointment setting and lead conversion. It all comes down to sets and runs. You will have an average result per run appointment. It is just like in Las Vegas with a slot machine. That slot machine generates an average amount per hour that it is sitting at the casino. If you look at all the money that was put in that slot machine, and then you deduct out all the money it paid out, and you did that for a whole year, you could calculate the profit of that slot machine per month, per week, per day, per hour, you could even go down to per second. There is so much that you can learn when you get clear on what these numbers are.

I had an e-mail from a client the other day that ran four appointments and did not make any sales. They were a little bit frustrated based on the level of effort that they put out. Part of my response back was, "Pat yourself on the back. You did a great job. Focus on activity, not results." When you take the right actions, you get the right results.

To be frank about it, in this economy, my numbers, my average revenue per appointment is down compared to last year. I am probably working harder this year than last year and not getting the same financial reward. That is okay. What we can control is our activity, and this is a time for you to be in action during the business day.

This is not a time to be in fear, panic and worry. That is not going to bring you money. Get yourself into action. Get your sales plan in place. Do the best you can to put your numbers together, and then just start paying attention to your numbers. The more you pay attention to it, the more you are going to learn about your numbers.

I was at a men's breakfast at my church about a month ago, and there was a gentleman named Paul Carroll who spoke, and he had written a book called, *Billion Dollar Lessons*. What he did was he studied the top 2,500 major business failures that he could find. And he looked at what the patterns were. What were the reasons why these businesses failed? One of the main reasons why there were these failures was the assumptions that the companies made. That was, to me, a profound thought. What are the assumptions?

I have a seminar coming up that I am doing as a free seminar. To put that event on it costs me about $5,000. I have to pay my staff, pay for the hotel, audio equipment, etc. I have committed to two days of training. And part of the reason that I was willing to take a $5,000 risk and two days of time is the assumption of the predicted revenue that will be generated. I made my assumptions based on the number of products and services I will be offering. And if my assumptions are right, then the event will be a profitable event. And if my assumptions are wrong, then it will not be profitable. Sometimes I am right and sometimes I am not. It is really important for you to look at your assumptions, and learn from them to ensure a successful future.

There are a lot of people that got in trouble with real estate. When they bought the real estate they made the assumption that the value will go up. The assumption was by the time the mortgage payment adjusts, "I can just refi out of it" or "I can just sell the property." There were a lot of assumptions that were made based on the real estate values and so forth, and as we all know, it turned out those assumptions were false. A lot of people lost a lot of money because they had made the wrong assumptions.

Start looking at what are the assumptions that you are making. What you assume is going to happen in your sales results is very, very important.

You can create a monthly plan, a weekly plan, and a daily plan. The system I use in tracking my results is simply based on using an Excel spreadsheet. What that means is, for a month like July, on the left-hand column in Excel, I would have 1, 2, 3, 4, as I go down those cells, all the way down to 31. And then on the right side, up at the top, I would have the categories I am tracking: Calls made, appointments set, appointments run, revenue collected. At the bottom after the number 31 for the month of July I would have a total, and I would do an auto summation for each column.

Next to the total I have my goal. So I can look at this Excel spreadsheet and see where I am at, at all times. Where I am at with my numbers versus what my goals are. Am I on track or am I off track? Arvee Robinson, a client of mine, will send me her tracker quite consistently. There was a month where she had a goal to hit $10,000 in a month outside of hitting a lot of revenue from her live seminars. It is the grind-it-out sales; day-to-day; belly-to-belly; phone selling; that kind of selling. She had a goal to do $10,000, and it is the first time she hit it that way, and she hit it around the 17th of the month. She was really excited. I looked at that and I was coaching her, and I said, "Arvee, do not stop. Your brain's going to say, woo-hoo, I hit my goal. I am going to rest. And I said, you need to go for 20. You are at the mid-way point of the month." So I was able to coach her based on what her tracker said.

Here are some things to consider when creating your plan. How many calls will you make? How many appointments will you set? How many appointments will you run? What are your expected results? If you are in network marketing, you will want to have personal goals that you are tracking, and then team production. So track it in two different ways. In separate lists track your personal production and then team production. You will want to spend some time over the next seven days creating your sales plan as it relates to the numbers. How many calls, how many appointments, how much revenue.

How To Generate Leads

$$\boxed{3}$$

The ultimate key to lead generation is the implementation of systems. The establishment of a never ending supply of leads is dependent on the development of multiple lead generation systems. If I were coaching you right now, I would ask you to share with me your lead generation systems. If you can only list one or two systems or none at all, we know where the problem lies.

Recently I was at the corporate headquarters for Infusionsoft. They are my database solution. They are the hub of my company and I decided to do some onsite training to learn how to optimize the database that I have. I have had the program now for about five years and I have never optimized it. The reason I am optimizing it is because that is what I believe is required for this economy. The way you win in this economy is optimization and that simply means you look at every aspect of your business and you ask yourself, "What can I do to improve it? What can I do to make it better?"

Lead generation begins with a database. Whether or not you use Infusionsoft, you absolutely have to have a database. I have been preaching this for years. This is not a should, it is a must (that is one of Tony Robbins' sayings, should's versus must's). Your database is an asset. For instance, the value of my database is in the millions of dollars. It is like a million dollar real estate portfolio or a million dollars in stock or a million dollars in the bank. It is why people like Brian Tracy have an interest in doing business with me. It is because of my database. And it is not just the size of the database; it is the connection I have with my database. I have added value for years and years to all my clients who are all over the world.

You want to build a database and build value with that database. With a database, the next step is to look for ways to leverage your database. One of the best ways to grow a business in any economy, including a down economy is to look for how you can introduce your database to other people and have them introduce their database to you.

In this book I have introduced you to Infusionsoft. Maybe you will want to talk to Infusionsoft and see if they are right for you. By the same token, Infusionsoft has been introducing some of their clients to me and I just picked up a brand new Platinum Protégé client. This is one of the ways that big business gets done. Think of Starbucks and Barnes and Noble; see how they are leveraging each other's networks.

The best leads that I have, number one, come from my house list. A house list is the people that are in your database. My second best leads are leads that I get by leveraging other peoples networks. So, when Infusionsoft introduces me to their network and then a lead comes over or John Assaraf (from *The Secret* fame) introduces me to his network or CEO Space does the same, these are my second best leads.

I have had a database for years and here it is five years after I started using Infusionsoft and I am finally optimizing it. So if you have not optimized your database do not feel bad, it is okay, but now is the time to step up your game, and optimize your database. Look for ways to leverage your database and look for people that you can work with synergistically and support each other through a concept I call a reciprocal referral relationship.

With Infusionsoft, obviously I believe in their company because I have been a client for five years now, so it is very easy for me to refer them. I am sure there are people that you can do business with and refer, just like I am referring Infusionsoft. These are people you would feel totally comfortable and confident referring to others, and you can ask them to reciprocate right back. If you build your database by two leads a day, twenty business days a month, that is forty leads a month. Over the course of a year, two leads a day, twenty business days a month, is four hundred and eighty warm market leads in one year. If you plan on being in business for at least ten more years, two leads a day over ten years is four thousand eight hundred warm market leads. That is easily within your grasp, to build a warm market database of forty eight hundred people over the next ten years.

I have been building my database now for about eight years and my list is almost up to thirty six thousand now. Whether you build it bigger than mine or not does not matter. What does matter is that you get into action now. What the database does it is provides a structure for you, so every time you get a lead you put it in the database.

The first thing that I do when I get back from a business trip and I have new leads, is I give them to my assistant and I say, "I want these leads to go into the database."

The inner game of lead generation refers to your mindset about leads. Do you believe that leads are abundant or do you believe that leads are scarce? What you believe about leads is very, very important. Go ahead and draw a circle in your notes right now. Then put a dot, just a little dot with your pen or pencil, in the center of that circle. Here's my belief, the circle represents opportunity, the opportunities that you have right now. The dot is how much opportunity you need to create in order for you to have overflowing opportunity. So you are at max capacity with that dot and the circle around it is the opportunity, and to me that is my metaphor about leads, abundance and opportunity. There are too many people that need my help, that is my mindset.

The outer game of lead generation refers to lead generation tactics. This deals with the how-to's of lead generation. Like your lead generation systems (i.e. your online lead generation system). Your lead generation scripts, your referral systems, your database, asking somebody for their business card, the networking meetings you go to, what you say at a networking meeting, these are all lead generation tactics.

Lead generation begins with identifying your target market. You need to identify your target market. Think about who is your market. Who do you service? I have diversified into quite a few different markets that I service. One of my markets is traditional sales people. These are people in businesses like; insurance sales, financial services, technology sales, inside sales or telemarketing. Then I have solo-preneurs like coaches and consultants. Another of my markets is small business owners. Another is network marketers. Those are the people that I am looking for. I am not looking for children, I am not looking for schoolteachers, and I am not looking for students. I am looking for people who are a natural fit with what I teach. When these people improve the quality of their communication and sales skills, they make more money.

Recently I have started doing more business training, especially in my Platinum protégé program. So by identifying business owners as one of my target markets I have been seeking out networks of business owners. That is why I am partnering up with a company like Infusionsoft because the people that use Infusionsoft, in most cases, are business owners. It is important for you to know who your target market is.

If you say that your target market is anybody, it is challenging to come up with effective lead generation tactics that attract anybody. Get clear on who is your market.

The POI

My number one lead generation idea, and if you just master this one idea you should have more leads than you can handle for the rest of your life, it is called POI. POI stands for Person of Influence, so you can jot this phrase in your notes; "I need to master Eric's POI strategy." Now, I have been teaching POI for many years and in the last six months even I have been able to get better at it.

Everyone in the world has a network. A POI is a person who has a network where a percentage of their network is in your target market. So think of someone who sells insurance and think of a real estate agent. So the real estate agent is a POI for the person who sells insurance. Because for the person who sells insurance, part of their target market is homeowners, and then the insurance person is a POI for the real estate agent, because many people who need insurance at some point would buy or sell a home.

In this example with the insurance agent and the real estate agent, they are both POI's for each other, and they can set up a reciprocal referral relationship. It does not just mean sending leads to each other. In a reciprocal referral relationship you are looking for ways to support each other. How can you help this other person, how can they help you? How can the two of you come together in the spirit of perfect harmony and support each other? Now imagine if you created ten reciprocal referral relationships.

I have many of these types of relationships. I have one with DC Cordova, Infusionsoft, John Assaraf, Brian Klemmer, Loral Langemeier and many, many other people. This form of lead generation is one of the big strengths for me and it can be for you as well! I have an ongoing stream of new leads coming in because I have built relationship with these people and I want you to know that you too can do this. If you will set the expectation to create ten reciprocal referral relationships, over time, you can do this. One place you can do this is on the sales champion community (www.SalesChampionCommunity.com). Many of the people in the sales champion are clients of mine and I have been teaching them about this concept. You might reach out to people in that community and tell them you are interested in talking about how you might be able to partner together to support each other.

Make a list of all of your potential reciprocal referral relationships. Then start contacting each one of them and discuss the mutual benefits of working together.

I was having lunch with this gentleman Ryan, who works for Infusionsoft. Ryan was talking about steps to take after the Sales Mountain that will increase your sales and leads. Remember, in the Sales Mountain the steps are; lead generation, appointment setting, trust and rapport, identify customer needs, share the benefits, start the close, objection handling and then ultimately you close the sale.

Ryan pointed out that there are steps after the close and follow-up. The first thing you do after you make the sale is you want to get your customer using your product. If they are not using your product then they are not going to buy from you a second time, a third time, a fourth time… After you close the sale, you want to be already thinking about how you are going to help your customer have the best experience possible by enjoying your product or service. Get them to use the product and then get them to be a testimonial. Then you want them to become a referral partner.

Just add that right onto the end of the Sales Mountain under Follow Up. As an example, say you close a sale today in your vitamin business. After they purchase the product from you, build into your system to check back in with them to make sure they are using the product and to see if they have any questions. And then help them to get so much value that they will give you a testimonial. Then ask for referrals. Now, you do not have to wait till then to ask for referrals but this is the system that will turn them into a referral partner. Now you will have a lead stream from this person, repeat business from them and referrals from them for life.

Now imagine your business like that. Let us say it took you twelve to eighteen months to build that and now the repeat and referral business is just pouring in. How exciting would that be?

• • •

Add To Your Database

The next idea is to ask people for their business cards. If you meet somebody and they are in your target market just say, "Would you like to exchange cards?" or "I would love to get your business card." Then once you get their card put it in your database. Giving them your card is not nearly as important as getting their card. You want to get their card because now you can have the opportunity to follow up with them. If you give them your card but do not get their card, now they are in control and they may never call you. Think of this like a video game. It is worth ten points to give them your card, and that is cool, but it is worth a hundred points to get their card

Use goal setting to build your database. You all know about goal setting. Set a goal for the number of leads that you want to have in your database. Now my company, we set a goal to double our database this year. We want to go to seventy thousand people by the end of the year. One of the ways that we are going to do it is with Google Ads and pay-per-click marketing. This is an online lead generation strategy. If you are not familiar with pay-per-click, just Google it and you can learn all about it. In a nutshell, you pay a small amount; it can be as minimal as twenty or thirty cents, every time somebody clicks on your link to go to your website.

My favorite way to generate leads is by doing public speaking or conference calls. I generate anywhere from five hundred to fifteen hundred leads per month doing public speeches and conference calls.

One strategy that almost all of you can do and I highly encourage you to do this, is to offer a free report on the Internet. Give the report away in exchange for the person's contact information. Here is a web site of mine that you can take a look at and use as a template, www.freesalesscriptingreport.com.

This is a huge, huge, huge idea that is generating thousands of leads. Online lead generation is crucial because people are frequently going on the Internet as a part of their buying process. So it is a way for you to acquire a lead, build your database, and then you can go back and market your product or service to them. In order to do this strategy you need an online database, and that is why I use Infusionsoft.

When you are on my website and you fill out a web form, you are actually filling out an Infusionsoft web form and going directly into my database. You will want to have the same thing. Offer something for free that adds value in exchange for the persons contact information. So if you are a real estate agent it might be a report on buying real estate at a discount. It might be a report on specific ways to increase the value of your home so you can get a higher price. Offer this report or an audio download or a webinar or whatever you are offering, in exchange for their contact information.

Video Marketing To Generate Leads

In the new economy, your web presence is becoming increasingly important. The last time you hired an insurance broker or financial planner or attorney; did you look up their website? Of course you did.

The language of the internet is turning to video. This trend is accelerating as the costs have been lowered to an affordable level. It is now possible for any person to take advantage of the benefits of video and increase their web presence. I personally learned of the power of video on the internet when I was contacted by John Limbocker.

It was the Monday before a Sales Scripting Seminar that I was hosting on the following Saturday. John contacted me with a simple proposition, if he could get me on the first page of Google for the term "Sales Scripting" by the end of the week would I then allow him to address the seminar attendees on his strategies. I know a fair deal when I see one so I accepted his terms.

Within 24 hours, John had blasted various sales scripting videos of mine all over the internet and had 8 of the top 10 spots on Google for the term "Sales Scripting." If I remember correctly, by the end of the week he had my videos occupying every one of the top 10 spots!

To this very day I receive leads from Google because of the work John did. People are able to find my message when they are looking for help in the area of sales scripting.

If you are looking to implement this strategy, you want to start by creating several videos. One of the easiest ways to do this is to first make a list of the ten most common questions you get on your product, service, and industry. Next, you simply make a video of your answers to those ten questions. If you use the Flip video camera like I do to record your videos, it comes installed with software to upload your videos directly to YouTube and Facebook.

The reality is, when it comes to getting listed on the first page of Google, it takes a lot of knowledge on how to set things up correctly so that Google will place you in those coveted top spots. There is a whole industry that caters to helping businesses do this very task. It is called Search Engine Optimization or SEO for short. When I need help in this area, John is who I look to for expert assistance.

John has a service that he provides to business owners and sales professionals that teaches you what you need to know to get listed on all the major search engines. It is called

SEODominators.com. As a favor to me, John will waive the $497 upfront investment when you use "lofholm" (without the quotes) in the coupon field. I encourage you to contact him through his web site and see what he can do for you.

How To Set Unlimited Appointments

4

There are three ways to increase your appointment setting results. First, there is the inner game, second, the outer game and third, the action of appointment setting.

The inner game of appointment setting is your mind set regarding appointments. It is your belief systems about appointments; it is your comfort zone. The outer game is the how-to's. It is your scripts; it is your system for keeping track of the appointments; it is how you confirm your appointments; it is the database that you enter them into; it is the how-to's. The third component is action. Moving yourself to follow through and take action and do what you know you should be doing in your business.

Now, there is an interesting thing about the inner game, the outer game and the action. Your mind set about appointment setting is very, very important. And if there was one area that I would say the majority of sales professionals have an opportunity to improve, it is in their mind set around what is possible. Even in a down economy, it is raining success around us all the time. It is a matter of having an expectation for success and being able to recognize it when it is there. There is tremendous opportunity for you to set appointments right now. Your script may need to change. You can tell when this is necessary if you are trying to set appointments and you are not being successful. You then know your script is not connecting with the audience.

I received an email from a Protégé this week and he was talking about doing seminars in his local market. He shared all these tactics that he was doing to fill up the seminars. And yet, with all that activity, there were only two people that showed up for the seminar. It is not that seminars do not work; it is that the marketing message did not connect with the potential participants.

What sells all the time, including during a down economy, is value. But what has changed for people is what they perceive as valuable.

In your appointment setting, you have got to look at your presentation from the customer's viewpoint. So you contact somebody and you want to book an appointment with them. You want to look at it through their eyes. What is the stand-alone value that the prospect is going to receive if they agree to meet with you?

In the training industry, content is king, and in sales, value is king. If you become a value-added resource for your clients and communicate that in the appointment setting process they will realize if they spend time with you they are going to receive value. If a prospect ever tells you they do not have the time, rarely is that true. We always find the time to do the things that are most important. One of the examples that I have shared in numerous seminars is if you are talking to a prospect and you say, "Would you like to book an appointment with me?" and they say, "Well I do not have the time," and your follow up to that is, "Well let me share with you this promotion that my company is doing right now. If you can meet with me sometime in the next seven days at a time that is convenient for both of us for only 30 minutes, and there is no obligation to purchase my product, if you can do that, at the appointment I will deliver you a crisp $100 bill. Just out of curiosity, did any time slots open up for you over the next seven days?" And all of a sudden they have the time!

What happened is you increased the value. In this case you increased the value with cash. There is an imaginary teeter-totter that goes on in the mind of the prospect. And on one side of the teeter-totter is time. That is what you are asking for is time. And on the other side is value. Now if you are taking notes, I would like you to draw a teeter-totter in your notes, and write time on one side and write value on the other side. So what you have got to do is make the value side way more than the time that you are asking for. For example, if you are in network marketing and you have a business opportunity meeting that is held at the local hotel on Wednesday night, and you ask somebody to come down to the meeting, you are asking them to give up their Wednesday evening to come to the hotel meeting. What they are probably going to do is watch television on Wednesday night. So you are asking them for their time and (I am not trying to be funny) they have a really high value on their TV watching. People place a lot of value on that. What you have got to do is convey value.

One way to convey value is with possibility. People will do a lot for possibility. When I do a free conference call, and people come to the call, they are coming to the call for the possibility that they are going to learn information that is going to help them sell their product or service. So if you are in network marketing and you are inviting them to a hotel meeting, what you create as a possibility is that their financial life is going to change for the better.

Regardless of what industry you are in, ask yourself this question, "When you meet with a prospect, what possibilities get created?" And then look for ways to convey that in the appointment setting presentation. If one were to look at the recent marketing emails that I sent out for my Ultimate Selling Power seminar, I used the idea of possibility. When you attend the program, it is going to create the possibility that you are going to increase your sales results every month for the rest of your life. Always remember that people will do a lot for possibility.

The 3 vital elements to a sales mindset are as follows:

1) There are more appointments that can be set than what you can possibly run. This is a fact. Especially in this economy because you have less competition. Whatever your product or service is, there is more appointments that you could go out on.
2) There are too many leads.
3) Appointment setting is fun and easy.

What is the language that you use? Start paying close attention to what is your language about life? What is your language when you talk about your kids, your spouse, your health, spirituality, or in this context, appointment setting? Is your language saying it is tough to get appointments? Everybody I meet with is not qualified. Or is your language that appointment setting is fun and easy.

Avoid saying, appointment setting is hard. I am not good at appointment setting. Or I am not good at sales. Your outcome when you set an appointment is to set an appointment. It is not to sell your product or service. When you deliver the appointment, that presentation is designed to sell the product or service. But the actual appointment setting, the purpose of it is simply to set an appointment, and that is a key distinction. This is stage selling and this is something in my philosophy that you will hear over and over and over again. You simply sell to the next stage. As you are working with your prospect, just ask yourself, what is the next step? If the next step is appointment setting, then your outcome of that appointment setting presentation is to schedule the appointment.

Oftentimes the appointment will cancel. When I used to work for Tony Robbins, I had a roommate. The way it worked was that since you lived on the road, and to save on expenses, you would share an apartment with somebody else on the team. So I had this roommate, and this guy would go ballistic when his appointments would cancel. It seemed like a tremendous amount of energy got exerted. He was just so frustrated and upset and angry when these appointments would cancel. And what I learned is to not become frustrated or upset when normal, natural things happen. An appointment cancelling is a totally normal part of the sales process.

Benefits of the Appointment

The benefits of the appointment are different than the benefits of your product and service. There are stand-alone benefits to the prospect meeting with you, whether they buy from you or not. You must communicate those stand-alone benefits in your appointment setting presentation to attract the prospect to want to meet with you.

If I was a real estate agent, one of the things that I would communicate is that the time of the appointment would be done at a time that is convenient for them. That is a benefit. During the appointment I will deliver a market analysis. That is a benefit. I will share my vision of how I would market their property. That is a benefit. They will have the opportunity to hire me at the end of the meeting. That is a benefit.

What happens, if you are doing a one-call close? A one-call close means that you are going to go on the appointment and you are going to ask for the order at the end of the presentation. If you are doing a one call close, what has to happen when you set the appointment is you have to manage the expectations of the call or the appointment. You want to let them know, when I come and meet with you, there is going to be a sales presentation, and I am going to be asking you for the business. But you cannot just come out and say it like that. You have got to do it in a way that is elegant. You want to let them know, I am going to close, but I am going to do it in an elegant way.

If you have ever heard me sell on a conference call, part of my formula at the beginning of the conference call is I always state the two outcomes that I have for the call. "My first outcome is to share some great ideas on scripting (if that is the topic). My second outcome is to extend an invitation for you and I to enter into a mentoring relationship and I will give you all the details on that at the end of the call." That is my elegant way of saying, "I am closing at the end of the call."

The reason why you want to do this is that it is very important that the prospect understands what is going to happen during that presentation. I had somebody contact me one time, and they said, "Eric, I would love to meet with you and share with you some great ideas on how to grow your business."

I was like, "I like great ideas." (And by the way, that is a great script. If you can truly deliver great content or great ideas, incorporate that into your appointment setting presentation.)

This guy framed it that he was going to give me all these great ideas. And I went out to meet him, and I mean literally, two-thirds of the way through the presentation he says to me, "Have you ever heard of a company called Amway?"

My response was, "You have got to be kidding me!" Now do not misunderstand me. I love Amway. I have trained many people from Amway. I was very frustrated with the particular tactic that was used to set an appointment with me. We want to create harmony with the prospect and we want to manage expectations.

What you could say if you are a real estate agent is, "After we meet and I deliver the market analysis and how I would market your property, you will have the opportunity to hire me as your real estate agent if you feel comfortable. And if not, then no problem, fair enough?"

The language is, "at the end of our time together, you will have the opportunity to hire me as your real estate agent, if you feel comfortable. And if not, then no problem, fair enough?" And what you are telling them is there is a closing, but I understand that you do not want to be hard sold to so I am not going to use hard sell, high-pressure techniques when I go to close. (And all I mean by close is you are just simply going to ask them to take the next step.)

The close is the natural conclusion to a well-delivered sales presentation.

Setting Up The Follow-up Appointment

When the next step in the sales process is a follow-up appointment, here is how you would schedule that:

Let us say you are doing a consultation, and then you want to schedule another time to speak with them to complete the sales process. One thing that you could say is: "We are getting towards the end of the call. What I would like to do now is share with you how we work with clients like yourself. Today we have done our initial call, and the next step is for us to schedule a follow-up call at a time that is convenient for both of us. On that follow-up call, what you can expect is blank, blank, blank. Go ahead and grab your calendar, and let us pick a time that is convenient for both of us."

It is just an assumption close. What you can do to take it one step further is say to them, "Now I have blocked this time out, so I will be calling you. If for any reason you are unable to meet at this time, if you can e-mail me 24 hours in advance, I would really appreciate it." Just let them know this is how you do it.

Selling is about leading. What happens in sales is you get to tell them how it works at your company.

How Do You Find The Right Contact

A common question I receive is, "If we do not know anybody in a company that we want to approach, how do we find the right people to talk to?"

LinkedIn.com is a great way to go. Also you could use the company website. A lot of times they list people on the company website. Lastly you could ask the person that answers the phone (if somebody live answers it). The script that you can use in this situation is as follows: They say, "XYZ Company, how may I direct your call?"

"Yes, my name is Eric and I am looking to get to the person in charge of blank. If you were me, what would you suggest that I do?" People love to help!

How To Deal With The No-Show Appointment

Using the example that you booked a phone appointment and the person was not there (or a face-to-face appointment with the same result). They did not contact you to cancel. How soon would you call back to set another appointment and what would you say?

I would leave a message at the missed appointment time. I would then call them the next day. I would use guilt (not in a bad way). I would say, "Hi, this is Eric. I was calling for Barbara. Barbara, I left you a message yesterday. We had a scheduled appointment and you were not there. I have not heard back from you. I want to make sure that everything is okay. Please call me back."

If you leave a really pleasant message like that, there is a great possibility that you are going to get a return phone call. You never know what is going on with people. All we see is what we see. You do not really know what is going on with people. Even with some of your neighbors you do not know. This person that you had this appointment with, they may be facing foreclosure on their house, or they might be going through a divorce or their kid might be addicted to drugs. You just never know. They might be about to get fired from their job. Just continue to call them and always stay in rapport when you do your follow-up phone calls.

• • •

How To Set Speaking Appointments

The way that you get speaking engagements is; it starts with lead inventory. Make a list of potential places that you could speak. Then the next step is to reach out and start contacting those people. Think of it from the viewpoint of the person booking the speaker. If you contact the chamber of commerce, somebody is in charge of booking speakers. You want to think like them and communicate the value that they are going to receive by having you as a speaker.

How do we get the prospect to commit to a time for your speaking engagement? When you do the free consultation you can tell a story during your front-of-the-room talk of a client for whom you did the free consultation and they then started working with you. What are the results that they received? You want the audience thinking, "Wow, I really want what that other client received."

If you are offering the free consultation to the participants at your speaking engagement, frame it properly. Here is something that I will say, "When you sign up for this free consultation, I want you to bring your biggest sales challenge to the call. And on the call I am going to put my brain to work on that biggest sales challenge. I will help you create a breakthrough during that 30-minute call." That is creating a lot of value to the prospect and clearly indentifies what they are going to receive from the free consultation.

How To Set Appointments From Radio & TV Advertisements

I was talking with a real estate guru this past week, and he does radio ads. The ad is for a free CD. What he wants to do is when the customer calls up for the free CD, he wants to upsell them at the point of contact. The problem is the expectation of the prospect. The prospect is just calling to get the free CD. The challenge is to try and sell that prospect something when they are not expecting a sales presentation.

When the phone call comes in the script will look like this: "Hello?"

"Yeah, I just heard you on the radio, and I want to get my free CD."

"Fantastic. Let me get your name, your phone number, your mailing address and your e-mail address. (get the information) Okay, great. Now there are two ways that we can get you this information. The first way is I can e-mail you an audio download, and you get instant access to it. The second way is I could mail you a CD. And if I mail you the CD, we do not charge you for the CD, we simply ask you to help with the shipping and handling. It is $3.95. Which would you prefer?"

Most will take the instant download.

The script continues with, "Because you called in, you are eligible to receive a huge discount on our jump-start real estate program. Would you like to hear about the program?"

"Sure."

Then you go into the explanation of it. You only explain the jump-start program if the prospect says "Yes, I want to hear about it."

The reason that this is important is that if you start going into the sales upsell without asking for permission, the prospect might be like, "Hey what are you talking about? I am just calling for my free CD."

When you are asking for these questions to be answered, and you are asking everybody and there are some people that are not going to want to hear the upsell. That is

OK. They were not in the right frame of mind to buy anyway.

How To Close The Sale

5

When you have the right system, the right formula, closing the sale is simple, easy and effortless. Even if you have anxiety around asking for the money, or you are uncomfortable asking for the order, I want you to know that with this system, you can break through that hesitation.

Barry Bonds is famous for steroid use. He is also famous for holding the record for most home runs in the history of baseball. This means that whether you like Barry Bonds or not, he has a really valuable mindset that can help you to be more successful with selling. I listened to an interview with Barry Bonds one time, and the person interviewing him said, "Barry, when you are up to bat, and you hit the ball perfectly, and it goes right to the second baseman for an out, does not that frustrate you?"

And he replied, "No. Why would it frustrate me?"

"Well, I mean, you just hit the ball perfectly and you got out and you are trying to get on base."

Bonds said, "Actually, I am not trying to get on base."

"Really, what are you trying to do?"

"My job when I go up to bat is to have a quality at-bat. So my whole focus is on making contact, quality contact with the pitch. And as long as I do that I have done my job."

As I listened to Barry Bonds share that on the radio, I decided to apply that to my selling. When I sell, my job is not to make the sale. That sounds kind of funny. What do you mean it is not to make the sale? My job is to deliver a quality presentation from the heart and ask for the order. As long as I have done that, I have done my job. What that does is it takes all of the pressure off of selling for me. It helps me with my confidence, in my inner game, knowing that I do not have to convince this person to buy from me. I am looking for the people that are already interested. So I put my focus in delivering a quality presentation.

What is the close? It is the section of the sales presentation where you ask for commitment. The close is the natural conclusion to a well-delivered sales presentation.

I had a sales presentation earlier today that I delivered on a conference call. I had almost a hundred people on the line, and my call to action at the end was for a $47 product. So I prepared by thinking through that presentation, because I knew what I was going to say, when I was going to say it, how I was going to say it and why I was going to say it. My sales presentation included a call to action. This is a critical piece to my formula for selling and my formula for closing. When I get to the close, it is kind of like an actor reading the lines for their part. Imagine you are in a play, and it is your turn to share your lines, and then you just share the lines. When you get to the close, your lines are letting the prospect know what the next step is.

Even if you are somebody who is a superstar closer, prepare your close in advance. Look for how you can optimize the close. When you do this it gives you tremendous confidence. What a lot of people do when they get to the close is they become uncomfortable and their speech rate changes. They start speaking faster or in a higher-pitched voice, because they are uncomfortable in the close. When you do what I am suggesting, you will become more confident.

If there is room for improvement for you in the area of closing, I want you to create an expectation right now that you will learn how to become a master closer. The way that you implement this is you get trained by somebody who is a master closer. While you are reading this book, that person is me. I was trained by three master closers; Dante Perano, Tony Martinez, and Dr. Moine. I do not know how many master closers there are on the planet. Let us say there are 5,000 of them, and 3 of the top 5,000 personally trained me. Now I am training you. I am transferring over the information from me over to you, and I want you to create an expectation that you become great at closing. You can do this because you are being trained by somebody who teaches people how to become great at closing.

Part of our results has to do with our self image. How we view ourselves. I want you to view yourself as either a great closer or somebody who is great at enrolling, or someone who is becoming great at those things.

In my system, the way you close is to decide before the presentation starts how you are going to close. Think of the presentation in reverse order, from the end to the beginning. In other words, keep the end in mind. I cannot stress that enough. Think about the next presentation that you are going to go on, and know that presentation backwards and forwards, inside and out. When you do this, you will close at a higher rate, you will become more confident. The way that you get better at playing the piano is you practice. The way that you get better at sales and at closing and delivering presentations is you practice. Every day you get a little bit better. Even at my level, every day I get a little bit better. The more presentations you deliver, the more successful you will become. You cannot deliver your 50th presentation until you have delivered your 49th presentation. The good news is every time you give a presentation, even if you do not close, you get a little bit better. Just keep delivering your presentations. Imagine how the close is going to go for you on your next presentation. Think about how you are going to explain the next steps. Decide in advance what you are going to say in the close. Practice, practice, practice.

The most successful people that I have ever met in closing do the same thing over and over and over again. I watched Dante Perano deliver about 50 front-of-the-room presentations. Every time he closed, he did it the exact same way. And the results were the same. Human beings respond in patterns. When you find a pattern that moves people to action, you can repeat the steps over and over and over again and move many people to action.

When I sold on my conference call today it was a presentation that I had never delivered, but I followed my formula for closing. On a conference call, the sales presentation consists of the intro, the outcomes, deliver the content, and then give a clear call to action directing people to the website or to call a phone number. I knew exactly how I was going to close. There is no guesswork. It is a system. Selling is a system. Closing is a system. I am a systems sales trainer. The beauty is, once you get this system down, you just do the same thing over and over and over again. Embrace the idea that selling is a learnable system and equals service.

Selling is about leading, selling is about moving people to action, so embrace sales. Embrace sales scripting.

Scripting is the main formula that I use for closing, and all scripting is, is deciding in advance what you are going to say. That is all it is. You do not want to do improv during your sales presentation. Comedians deliver their presentation and they know what jokes they are going to tell. They are delivering their routine. There are certain comedians that have an amazing routine and they just go from city to city and everybody loves it. And there are other comedians that do improv. With improv, we do not know if it is going to be funny or not. Even the great Jim Cary said that when he did improv, in many cases he got booed off the stage when he was early in his career. Improv is done in small comedy houses. Comedians that travel from city to city deliver their presentations to large audiences in great halls. That is the difference between scripting and improv.

Before you read this chapter, you might have done improve (another name for improv is winging it). Always remember that when you wing it, you get wing-it results. If you used to wing it, that is okay. But now you are being trained by an expert. I am training you to prepare.

When you deliver your script I want you to know you can absolutely be authentic and you can be flexible and you can come from the heart. Simply prepare and know how you are going to close. That is the key to closing greatness. It is your level of preparation. The definition of a script is simply words in sequence that have meaning. Many people resist scripts because they do not want to sound canned or rehearsed, or they believe a script is beneath them. However, I did not say it had to be rehearsed. A script is simply words in sequence that have meaning. So I am giving you the freedom to come from the heart, be yourself, and then at the same time, powerfully move people to action with your products and services.

I use scripts because they work. They are good for me; they are also good for the customer or client. Scripts are the easiest, most effective way to move someone to action.

Scripts have two components. They are; language and structure. The language part includes; the words, your tonality, the speech rate, body language and pausing. The structure part is the order of the script. It is the sequence. Remember the metaphor of having a meal at the Olive Garden.

Remember the process we discussed earlier about going to the Olive Garden restaurant. When you go to the Olive Garden, they say, how many in your party? They give you a coaster that lights up when your table is ready. Once you sit down, they say, can I start you off with a beverage? Would you like an appetizer? What would you like for your entree? They bring you the food. They ask you how your meal was. They offer you dessert, they offer you coffee, and then they bring you the bill. The bill always has the green Andes mints. And here's what is fascinating. If all of us right now, whatever town you are in, if you have an Olive Garden or a restaurant like it, if you went there right now, that is exactly what would happen. Well, think about in your sales presentation. If you had it mapped out like that, where at first you did this and then you did this, and then you did that, and you just knew it. You knew it backwards and forwards, inside and out. Think about how confident you would feel.

Now one of the things about a sales presentation that you cannot fake is preparation. When you are live with the prospect, you operate at whatever level of practice you put in. If there is something that is worth putting your time, effort and energy into, it is figuring out what should be in your presentation and then practicing it. It is been said that sales superstars out-earn people that are average in sales by a factor of 10:1. It does not mean those superstars are working ten times harder. They are more efficient and effective because they are delivering a much more effective sales presentation.

The example of an effective presentation is the Sales Mountain. You can go back and reread that chapter. The Sales Mountain process, just like the process at the Olive Garden, it is all about trust and rapport, identify customer needs, share the benefits, close, objection handling, close and follow-up. So that is the step-by-step process, just like having a meal at the Olive Garden.

Closing Techniques

Selling is a thinking man's game.

One technique is called contrasts.

At Carl's Junior, the fast food restaurant, they have a burger, and it is called the $6 Burger. But they do not sell it for $6. I think they sell it for about $4. What they are doing is, they are saying "If you go to a hotel, and you order a hamburger, you are going to pay about six bucks. We'll give you the same hamburger at Carl's Junior for four dollars." It has been very popular. It is been around for several years (when they started offering the burger the competition was selling theirs for $6, now it is more like $10). That is using the technique of contrasts.

I was going through a real estate magazine yesterday, and in the magazine it said, one million dollar home for $775,000. Well, that does not really make sense. If it is a million-dollar home it would be a million dollars. But what they are saying is that the value of the home is a million, but you can pick it up for 775. That is different than saying the home is $775,000. It is using contrasts. Think about how you can use contrasts in your selling. When you go to the close section of your presentation, look for how you can use contrasts in that section of the presentation. And once you get it down, write it down. If you do not write it down, over time you might forget it. Then this really great killer technique in your close, it is just slipped out because you forgot about it.

The next technique is a preframing technique. Preframing simply means to let somebody know in advance what is going to happen. A financial planner might say, "For me to best help you, I need you to have your taxes from the last two years ready for our appointment. Can you have that ready?" And that would be done during the appointment setting part of the presentation. That is a preframe. When I used to work for Tony Robbins, I was selling seminar tickets. I would be in a city like Atlanta, Georgia. I would go into a real estate office, and I would deliver a free training presentation. At the end of the training there was a call to action for the Tony Robbins tickets. Well, here is what would typically happen. If I did not preframe how the meeting was going to happen, I would get to the end of the presentation and say, "Tickets are $299. Fill out the form."

Then they might turn around and look at the real estate broker and say, "Hey is the company going to pay for it?"

Then if I did not preframe it, the broker would say, "Well I do not know. I have not thought about it."

Then the person would say, "Well Eric, when we find out what the company is going to do, then we will let you know what we are going to do."

Well that happened to me a few times, and so I started preframing it. When I set the appointment up, I would say to the broker, "Now when I get to the end of the presentation, I need to share with all of your agents how much the seminar is going to cost. And they are going to want to know if you are going to pay for it or not. So how about you and I get on the same page so we can deliver a clear, consistent message to your team. Sound good?"

And the guy or gal might say, "Yeah, that sounds good."

"Okay, so, do you want to pay the $299 for each of your people, or do you want to split it with them, or do you want them to pay on their own? Of those three, which would work best for you?"

"I will split it with them."

"Okay, so how does that work? If they decide they want to do it, does that mean that they will put all of it up and get reimbursed back? Or does that mean that you will put all of it up and then they will pay you half, or pull it out of a future commission?"

They might say, "Well, how about the agents put the money up first, and then I will reimburse them."

So then when I get to the close, I say, "Now the tickets are $299, and Bob the Broker, you want to share with the group what the company is going to do?"

"Yeah, we are going to pick up half of the ticket cost."

"Let us give Bob a big hand. So how this is going to work is each of you, you are going to pay the full $299 today, and then you will get a receipt and you will turn that in to Bob for reimbursement."

See, that is a preframing technique. Here is the beautiful thing. When I walk into that presentation, I already know exactly when I am going to turn it over to Bob to share what the company's willing to do. I know how I am going to take back control of the meeting. I know how I am going to explain to them how the price split is going to work and how they are going to get reimbursed back. Do you see the power of that? I want you to know, if you are not at that level yet, you can get to that level.

One of my favorite preframing techniques is to say, "I have two outcomes for my presentation. My first outcome is to share some great ideas with you. My second outcome is to share with you, how my ongoing coaching program works and I will give you all the details of that at the end of the meeting.

On your next presentation you might say to your prospect early on, "I have two outcomes for my presentation today. My first outcome is to share with you some great ideas on _____ (fill in the blank). And my second outcome is to share with you all the details in how we can work together beyond today's presentation. And I will give you all the details on that at the end of our meeting today." See, what happens when you use a preframing technique like that is you are managing the expectations of the presentation. You are letting the prospect know that you are going to give value and there is going to be an offer made at the end. It is an elegant way of saying that you are going to close.

Using Silence To Close

When I sell one-on-one, I always ask for the order, and then I am silent. I use this technique 100% of the time. I get to the end of the presentation and there is a distinctive section called the final close. And the final close, when you are selling one-on-one, it is this sentence that you say when you ask for the order. "How do you feel about moving forward? Are you ready to take the next step?"

"We can do a two-month supply or a three-month supply. What would work best for you?"

When I say the final close, then I am silent. Part of the language of influence is silence.

Alternate Choice Close

"We can get you started with the gold package or the platinum package. Which would you prefer?" That is an alternate choice close.

"I am looking at my calendar. I am available on the 2nd or the 9th. What would work best for you?" This is another alternative choice question where you give the prospect two or more choices where the answer to both choices is a yes. In the alternate of choice, you are not asking them if they want to do it, you are assuming that they want to do it.

"We accept Visa, American Express, MasterCard or Discover. Which credit card would you like to use today?"

"We could do a three month or a four month listing. What would work best for you?"

"We can do a 15-year or a 30-year loan. What would work best for you?"

"You can buy one month of service or 12 months. If you buy 12 months, you will receive a 20% discount. What will work best for you?"

The Order Form Close

This is where you give the prospect an order form and walk them through the form. They have the form in front of them and you go through it with them.

"Just put your name down right here, and go ahead and jot down your mailing address. And then you can put your credit card in here." When I sell from in front of the room, I do not always do this, but many times, I will put an order form in the hand of all the participants and I will just walk them through the form.

"On the form where it says $1295, cross out $1295 and write in $299. Go ahead and do that for me now please." I am giving a direct command. Human beings respond to direct commands. And when I do this, people cross out $1295 and they jot down the $299 price. The power of this is that the prospect starts writing on the registration form. I am effectively leading and as you know by now, selling is about leading. Selling is about moving people to action.

"And then write down plus bonus CD set, because everyone that registers today will receive a copy of this CD set as a free bonus. Where it asks for your e-mail address, jot down your e-mail address. Where it asks for your credit card, go ahead and jot down your credit card." Now at this point, the audience realizes I am closing. But it is done in a way that they are not feeling pressured. It is their choice. What is great about a close like this is that if somebody wants to do it, they are going to do it. You are making it clear, compelling and you are leading them to what that next step is that you want them to take.

And if they are listening to you and you say, "Put down the credit card" and they do not want to do it, then they just will not put down their credit card. That is fine. No problem. You want the close to be clear and compelling.

Selling is about leading.

Most people are silently begging to be led. Every one of you reading this book would like it if I would lead you to sales greatness.

When I work, I am a client for somebody. If I am working with a real estate agent and they are helping me, I want them to lead me to real estate greatness. I want them to sell my home at a great price in the shortest amount of time. I want them to go out and negotiate a great purchase price for me. When you work with a professional you are looking to them for guidance. Many times when I hire somebody to do a service for me, they will ask me, "What do you think we should do?"

And I will ask them, "Well, you tell me. You are the expert. I came to you because you are the expert. Lead me."

People are silently begging to be led.

The Trial Close

"If I can reduce your monthly payments and get you $10,000 in cash at the close, would you like to refinance your mortgage?" In a trial close you are asking for a minor agreement. You are not actually asking for the sale at that point. This is called a trial close.

Ask.

"Would you like to go to lunch today?" That is just simply asking. Do not underestimate the power of asking, especially if you follow asking with silence.

The Sympathy Close

"It would really help me out if you could buy some cookies from my daughter for the Girl Scouts. Most people are buying five boxes. Could you buy at least two?" Notice we are using contrasts there. "Most people are buying five boxes. Could you buy at least two?" Do not underestimate the sympathy close. It is a very, very persuasive close.

The Leverage Close

This is a common technique used with collection agencies. They call you up and they point out the consequences if you do not pay. "Your interest rate and your fees are going to continue to go up, your credit is going to be impacted; you may have a hard time buying a home in the future because your credit score goes down."

What they are doing is they are pointing out the consequences of not doing what they are suggesting. That is the leverage close.

Assumption Close

"Which credit card would you like to use today?"

"How much did you want to start investing today?"

"What would be the best day to have our medical people stop by the house to do the testing for your life insurance?"

Scarcity Close

"We only have one left. Would you like to get it?"

Where true scarcity exists, you want to absolutely use this tactic because human beings respond to scarcity. It is a very powerful close.

You do not want to misuse the technique. Only use it where true scarcity exists.

I recruited a guy named Brian to work for me a little over a year ago. What I shared with Brian is I said "Brian, I am looking for somebody to do joint ventures for my company. And I have that opening today, and you are my first choice. So I would like you to come on board and do joint ventures for me. Now, I also want you to know, I only need one person. And if for any reason you do not want this position, then I am going to go and recruit and find somebody that does want it. So Brian, if you choose not to accept this position today or in the near future, and you come back to me two months from now, I will absolutely have a place for you on my team, but I will not have this opportunity to do joint ventures, which is a very excellent commissioned opportunity."

I pointed that out to Brian. It was true. I had one spot available. If he did not take it, I was going to find somebody else to do it, and he took action on it. I enrolled Brian by pointing out true scarcity.

The big idea of this chapter is to prepare your presentation in advance and specifically, know how you are going to close. You need to take action on that even if you are already a master closer. If you spend more time preparing and then implementing these techniques, you will improve and go to the next higher level.

For those of you for whom closing is new to you, or you are uncomfortable with closing, I want you to know that you can become my next great success story.

How To Handle Any Objection

6

I am a systems sales trainer. I approach sales challenges by looking at how we can solve them using a system. A lot of people struggle with objections but when you follow a system, it can help you much more easily convert prospects to sales. When an objection comes up, oftentimes the prospect is this close to saying yes (I am holding my thumb and index finger where they are almost touching to emphasize how close they are). You have delivered this great presentation, you have asked the prospect to buy from you, and they give you an objection.

The price is too high. I need to think about it. I need to talk it over with my spouse. In many cases with just a little bit of discussion or encouragement, they will say "yes."

We are going to talk about step-by-step exactly how to do this. This is in an area of selling where first you learn the basics and then you learn the advanced techniques. Then the next level is mastery of the basics. When it comes to objection handling, this is something that you want to strive towards. This is called mastery of the basics.

Selling is a thinking man's game.

When you sell, look for angles.

Objection handling is all about looking for opportunities to help move the prospect to action. I am going to share with you some of the best ways that I know to do that. Again, what is nice about this is that this is a system. It is something that is simple. It is easy and it is something you can duplicate.

Those of you that have a recruiting component to your business, or you are a trainer or you are a manager of a team of people that sells, I want to remind you of the distinction of training the trainer. Take what you learn from this chapter, at least one idea or more, and share them with your team in the next seven days. That will then duplicate yourself in your team, but also, equally important, you will get what it is that I am sharing with you at an even deeper level.

There are typically 7-12 common objections in any industry, and that is great news. It is not 50 or 100. There are only 7-12. Because there are so few common objections, you can choose to improve your objection handling techniques and responses with relative ease. The first step is to identify the common objections in your industry.

Here is a list of several that are common to most industries:

> I need to think about it.
> I do not have any money.
> I need to talk it over with someone.
> Can you fax me some information?
> I do not have the time.
> Your price is too high.
> I am already working with someone.
> We already tried it and it did not work.
> I am not interested.

For your specific industry, there are probably some other objections in addition to those listed above. Begin by making a list of the common objections in your industry using my list as a template.

Do you remember the hot potato metaphor that I shared in the Sales Mountain chapter? The way that I sell when I am selling one-on-one is to ask for the order, and then I am silent. And I use that close on every single one-on-one presentation. You will deliver the close, ask for the order, and then you are silent. When I am silent it produces a predictable response. The prospect is going to say one of three things. They are going to say "yes", they are going to say "no", or they are going to give an objection. Prediction is a form of power. I probably used the closing strategy of asking for the order and being silent several thousand times. And 100% of the time, the prospect said "yes" or "no" or they gave an objection. So you can know what the prospect is going to say.

Remember there are only 7-12 common things that they can say and will say. Because of that, we can then develop powerful, well-prepared responses to move the prospect to action.

If you are getting connected to what I am sharing with you, all of a sudden you can now become a master at handling objections. The way you get better at playing the piano is you practice. The way that you get better at handling objections is you practice. What I am giving you is the exact system that I use.

When you get out with the prospect, you are going to be authentic with them, you are going to really listen to them and you are going to have all these responses that you have practiced to perfection and you will have them at a subconscious level.

The hot potato metaphor means, I ask for the order and I am silent. I give the prospect the hot potato. They say,

"I need to think about it." Now I have the hot potato. So what do I want to do? I want to give it back to them.

"Well tell me more about that."

And they say whatever it is that they say. Maybe they give me another objection. And then I respond, "Is that your only concern?"

Then they say "yes."

And I say, "Other than the price, is there anything else preventing you from moving forward?"

There is a natural banter that goes on back and forth, back and forth, between you and the prospect.

A couple of years ago I picked my son Brandon up from kindergarten. And my son got in the car and he said, "Dad, can we go to McDonald's today?" So he is closing.

And I said, "Not today, son." So when he said, "Can we go to McDonald's today?" he gave me the hot potato. And I said, "Not today, son." So do you think my son just said, "oh, okay." No! He said, "Come on, Dad."

"Brandon, we just went yesterday."

"Just this once?"

You see, there is a banter that was going on between my son and me. This is what happens in real world influence. I want you to be prepared for it, have great responses ready to go, so when you get to the close and you ask for the order and an objection comes up, you are coming from a place of power and confidence. You are not surprised by an objection. You are not in a place of anxiety over the objection. You just very calmly respond with your most powerful response. It does not mean that you are going to close every sale. I do not close every sale. But what you will start doing is you will start closing the sales that you should. You will start moving the people that you should be moving to action based on the quality of the presentation that you delivered, based on their true need for what it is that you are offering.

Objection handling is a form of negotiation. So here is what that means. If you went down to the car lot today at a dealership, and you test drove a car. You got to the end of the presentation, and the sales person said, "Would you like to buy the car?" And you said, "Maybe, how much is it?" And they said "$30,000." Would you then say, "Great, I will take it?" No. You might say, "Well, I like the car, but not at $30,000. I was thinking more like $20,000." When you say $20,000, are you expecting the car sales person to say, "Great, I will go let my manager now and we'll write it up?" You are not expecting that. You are expecting, when you say $20,000, which they are going to then counter with, "No, $30,000 is the best we can do", or they are going to say, "Oh, we could do $27,500 if you buy it today."

What is key about what I am sharing is that when you go to a car lot, unless it is a lot like Car Max or Saturn where the price is the price, you expect a negotiation, some banter back and forth between you and the sales person. Objection handling is no different.

If you go into the presentation with an expectation that it is very possible they will provide you an objection, you will not be surprised by it. You will have responses to come back with, and you will be much more confident, much more effective and you will close a lot more sales. Now those of you that have a team of people, and you are going to be training them, you will want to role play these techniques. If you do not have a team, for yourself you will want to role play these techniques. You want to find somebody in your office, or a friend or a coach or whomever you can work with and say, "Will you role play some different objections? I am going to ask you for the order, and then you give me an objection, and then I am going to respond." When you practice this, when the live presentation comes up, you will be able to effortlessly move people to action.

When a prospect gives you an objection and you do not respond or you do not have an effective response, it communicates a message to your prospect. You are always in communication. What you say communicates. What you do not say, what you do, what you do not do – all of that is communication.

There are many ways to address these objections. Here are several different techniques. What is really cool about what I am going to share with you right now took me more than a decade to learn and you are going to get this information in this chapter. We are going right to the specific step-by-step objection handling techniques that close sales.

The Tools

Here are the tools to overcoming any objection:

1) Use a story.
2) Use a question.
3) Solve the problem.
4) Isolate the objection.
5) Bring out the objection.
6) Use a script.
7) Overcome before it comes up.
8) Investigative selling.

• • •

The Story

The idea is you want to learn multiple ways to handle the objection and then use whatever technique you think is going to best communicate with the prospect (or whichever one you remember at that time).

Let us talk about a story. One of the most powerful ways to handle an objection is with a story. The reason why stories are so persuasive is they act as invisible selling. Stories also suspend time. Identify true stories that address the objection. One way to start off a story is by saying, "That reminds me of a story of a client who was in a similar situation. Let me share with you what they did." So if you are talking to a prospect and they say "the price is too high" use a story that addresses what someone else did. For instance, if you have ever sold to somebody who also said the price is too high, but then eventually bought from you, you could tell that story.

You could say, "You know, that reminds me of a story of a client I was working with, and they had the same concern as you. They thought the price was too high. And what I shared with them was, benefit, benefit, benefit. And they said, 'You know, Eric, I would never think of it from that viewpoint. You know what? I want to go ahead and do it.'" You address the objection through a story of someone in a similar situation.

Ask a Question

The next technique is you can address an objection with a question. No matter what they say, you give them a question.

"The price is too high."

"By too high, what exactly do you mean?" And then you are silent. You just gave them back the hot potato.

"The price is too high."
"How much too high is it?"

"The price is too high."
"Compared to what?"

"I do not have the time."
"When will you have the time?"

"I do not have the time."
"On a scale of 1-10, how motivated are you to move forward?"

"I do not have the time."
"What do you mean by that?"

Here's another great question that works for virtually any objection. "Is that your only concern?"

When you are selling to a prospect, never use the word objection. "Objections," that is a sales training term describing the common reasons why somebody does not move forward. Instead, use the word concern.

Here is a sample close:

"How do you feel about moving forward?"
"You know, Eric, this sounds really great. I would love to. I need to talk it over with my spouse."
"Is that your only concern?"
"Yes."

"If your spouse says yes, does that mean you will move forward?"

"Yes I will."

That is a trial close. So no matter what they say, you say, is that your only concern.

Solve The Problem

The next way to handle an objection is to solve the problem. So an example of this is, if I was inviting somebody to a hotel meeting on a Wednesday night. And I said, "I would love for you to come down. We are going to have this great meeting and will you come?" That is the close, and then I am silent.

And they say, "Well Eric. I do not have child care." And I reply, "Well is the child care your only concern?"

"Oh, yeah, Eric. I would love to come. I just don't have anyone available to handle the child care."

"All right. So if I arranged for somebody to watch your children, whoever you use and I paid that babysitter, if I could make child care arrangements for you, would you come?"

And they say back, "Well yeah. If you could make child care arrangements, I would be there."

See, the sale closes by solving the problem. I have closed a lot of sales in that way. Sometimes when I am talking with a prospect, if they say, "I would love to do it. The price is fine but I just do not have the money today."

I might say, "Well, if we worked out a payment arrangement that was comfortable for you, would you like to move forward?"

And they say, "Well, what exactly would that look like?"

"Well, you tell me. What would be comfortable for you?"

"Oh, well I could do $200 a month for the next three months."

"Great, well let us do it."

Close the sale by solving the problem.

Isolate the Objection

The next technique is to isolate. Isolate the objection is one of my favorite techniques. I like it because it is very effective and easy to learn.

Objection: "I do not have the money."

Here's the language pattern. "Other than the money, is there anything else that is preventing you from moving forward?"

So it goes like this: Other than blank, is there anything else that is preventing you from moving forward? Fill in the blank with whatever the objection is.

"Eric, the price is too high."

"Other than the price, is there anything else that is preventing you from moving forward?"

"How do you feel about getting started today?"

"I need to talk it over with my spouse."

"Other than talking it over with your spouse, is there anything else preventing you from moving forward?"

That is the technique of isolate.

Bring Out The Objection

The next technique is to bring out the objection. It is a language pattern that goes like this: "I do not have the time."

"Other than the time, I am sure you have some other concerns before moving forward. Do you mind sharing what those concerns are?"

So instead of isolating the objection, you are encouraging more objections.

"I need to talk it over with my spouse."

"I can appreciate that, Barbara. Other than talking it over with your spouse, I am sure that you have some other concerns before moving forward. Do you mind sharing what those concerns are?"

We are encouraging an objection there. The reason why you might want to use a technique like this is if the prospect is saying something that it is not making sense to you. For instance, if they say, "I do not have the money," and maybe they drive a very fancy car and you are only asking them for a hundred dollar sale and they are balking about the money. Your inner voice is saying, this just does not add up. There is something more to what is going on. And so then you encourage them to object more. You create a safe space for them to share with you what is really going on.

Use a Script

You can develop scripted responses for each objection. Here's a script I have used that has closed many seminar tickets.

"How do you feel about moving forward?"

"Eric, I need to talk it over with my spouse."

"Okay, I can appreciate that. Let me ask you a question. If your spouse says 'yes' does that mean that you will move forward?"

"Yeah, absolutely."

"Fantastic. Well, what if your spouse says no?" They usually have not though it through. They have not really gone into their brain and thought, well, what if I talk to my wife or husband and they do not want me to do it. They have not thought it through to that level.

They just said, "I need to talk it over with my spouse." And when I say, "Well what if your spouse says no?" About 50% of the time they go ahead and do it anyway. I then reach over and I shake their hand, and I say, "Congratulations. You are going to have a great time at the seminar. Take a moment and fill out the rest of the form." And the sale closes.

That is a scripted response.

Overcome Before It Comes Up

Right now I am going to give you some very advanced content. This is a golden nugget. This is the kind of content that you would learn at a $5,000 boot camp. It is one of the most advanced ways to influence a prospect. What you do is, in the body of your presentation, you tell a story of somebody who had an objection. I will give you a real-world example, one that I regularly use. When I first met Arvee Robinson, she had a resistance to selling and a resistance to sales scripting. When I share her success story in the body of my presentation I bring out the fact that she had a resistance to scripting and a resistance to selling, which is true. And I was able to help her break through that and take her business to a whole new level. So what happens is, someone in the audience is listening and they say to themselves, "Wow, I can really relate to what Eric's saying." This is all happening on a subconscious level. Their inner voice says, "I have a resistance to selling. Wow, look at what it did for Arvee. Maybe this can have a similar result for me." So what we are talking about is strategically placing stories in the body of your presentation to address an objection before it comes up.

One time I was at a time share presentation. And the sales person said, "Now, at XYZ Company, the price is the price. We do not negotiate. We do offer same-day incentives. So if you choose to purchase today you will receive some incentives that will only be available if you purchase today." They said this very early on in the presentation. Now think about this. Why did they say that? They are knocking out the objection of negotiation, because they have delivered the presentation before, and if they do not say the price is the price, then the person might say, "Well, I would be willing to do it if you sold it to me at this price point." This is a preframing technique.

Remember, preframing is where you let somebody know, in advance, what is going to happen. What I am telling you right now, it is so important. Because as you improve the quality of your presentation, it is going to make you more effective, it will improve every presentation that you deliver for the rest of your life. This can put money in your pocket. This can help your clients enjoy the wonderful products and services that you offer by helping them make a decision.

Selling is a lot like mental chess. In chess you anticipate your opponent's move. In a sales presentation, you prepare, prepare, prepare. Anticipate what your prospect's concerns might be, and do your best to address them, either in the body of the presentation or after they come up. So when they preframe in the time share example, "the price is the price," it is unlikely that the prospect is going to say, will you do it for a lower price? It does not mean they will not, but it dramatically decreases the likelihood that they will bring up that objection. When they say, we offer same-day incentives, it eliminates the objection of, "I need to think about it." Because their same-day incentives are very compelling, and if the prospect wants to do it, it is likely that they will move forward today.

The Invisible Objection

This objection has cost you more money than all the other objections combined. It is the invisible objection.

The invisible objection is the objection that exists in your mind, not the prospect's mind. Let us say you are in financial services, and you meet somebody who is very financially successful and who would be a wonderful client for you. You talk yourself out of prospecting them by thinking, 'I am sure they already have a financial planner. They will not need my help.'

Or you are a real estate agent. And you are thinking about farming in your neighborhood, knocking on doors, letting people know that you are a real estate agent in the neighborhood, and instead of knocking on those doors, you think to yourself, 'they probably already have a real estate agent,' so you do not knock on the door.

Or for me, being in sales training, I could assume that somebody already has a great sales system in place, so I do not ask them if they need any sales training help.

Or if you are in network marketing, meeting somebody who is very successful, and just assuming that they would not have an interest in learning about your opportunity. That is the invisible objection.

It is possible you have left some of the best opportunities of your life on the table because you did not pursue them because you decided in your mind that they did not need your product or service. Always ask. Put yourself in a position to win. Present the opportunity. At the very least, ask them. If they say they are not interested, then they say they are not interested. Not a big deal.

Investigative Selling

I want to tell you about one of my star clients, Joe Amendola. When I was working with Joe he was selling air purifiers. He was talking with this one client, and he says, "Would you like to buy an air purifier?" (This is after he had delivered his presentation.)

And the guy said, "The price is too high."

Joe used an objection handling technique called investigative selling. Investigative selling is where you simply say, "Tell me more about that." No matter what they say.

I taught this to Joe and this is the real story. This is really what happened.

The guy says to Joe, "The price is too high."

Joe reply's (giving the hot potato back), "Well tell me more about that."

"Well, can I be honest with you?"

Joe of course says, "Yes."

"Actually it is not the price or the money, it is my wife."

"Tell me more about that."

The guy said, "I have two air purifiers in my garage and neither one of them work. And if I buy another one, my wife will be furious with me."

Now can you picture that scenario? I can completely picture it.

So Joe said, "Well where did you buy the air purifiers?"

The guy told him. Joe's response was, "Well, that is a reputable store. If the air purifiers do not work, I am sure they'd take them back. Why do not you give them a call and see if they will take them back. And if they are willing to take them back, then would you move forward and buy the air purifier from me?"

The guy says, "I guess so." So the customer called up the company and said that they did not work, and the company said that they would be willing to take them back. Joe followed up with him and closed the sale, using the technique of 'tell me more about that.'

Now in that example, the guy said it was the money. It was not the money. It was that he was concerned his wife was going to be upset with him. Oftentimes the true objection is what is called a non-stated objection. So the prospect does not tell you what the real issue is. That is why these techniques are so important.

The last story I want to share with you is about another one of my star clients named Mandy Pratt. I was teaching these techniques to Mandy. Remember when you banter back and forth with the prospect, the name I have for that is elegantly dancing with the prospect. No arm-twisting, no high pressure. You simply use the technique of elegantly dancing. You get to the end of the presentation and you ask for the order, then you are silent.

Mandy asked this prospect, "Would you like to buy the program?" Now she was selling a $6,000 wealth-building program over the telephone.

The prospect said, "I do not have the money."

And Mandy replied, "Tell me more about that."

The prospect said, "Well, I did a program like this before, and it did not work out. And my husband was really upset. So I am concerned that if I do this program, it will upset my husband."

Then Mandy inquired, "Have you talked to your husband about the program yet?" And she had not. Then Mandy said, "Well, how do you feel about putting your husband on the line, and the three of us can talk about it, and I will just simply share that you are interested in the program. Because of the bad experience you had in the past, you did not want to move forward until you spoke with him and found out what he thought about it. And then we will see what he says."

The woman said, "Okay, I will do that." So she went and got the husband, and now the three of them are on the phone.

Mandy says to the husband, "I am talking with your wife. There is this wonderful program coming up. She is interested. She wants to create more wealth for the family. She shared a bad experience that you and she had had with another company, and so we wanted to get your feedback. What do you think about her participating in the program?"

After Mandy shared the program with the husband, his reply was, "It sounds really good, so if she wants to do it that is fine." Mandy closed a $6,000 sale. Her commission on that was 20%. She made $1,200 on that one sale. The client was able to get involved with a great program to help her with her wealth building. That is why these techniques are so important.

Be Unreasonable

Now I am going to give you a bonus objection handling technique. It is called, be unreasonable. Now I am planting the seed with you, and there is going to be a time in the next 30 days and you are going to try this technique out and very possibly you will close the sale. And after you close the sale using this technique, you are just going to put a big smile on your face, and your inner voice is going to say, "I cannot believe that just worked!"

One time I wanted to go to a seminar called Money and You. And I wanted my wife to go to the seminar with me, and the seminar was coming up in two weeks. It was $2,000 for us both to attend. So I said to my wife, "Honey, I really want you to go to this seminar with me."

And she asked, "When is it?" I gave her the date. And she said, "I cannot do it."

"How come?"

"I have arrangements to fly up to the Bay area with the kids," we were living in San Diego at the time, "and I am going to go see your family."

And I responded, "Why not just go on a different weekend?"

"You do not understand."

"What is there to understand?"

"These are non-refundable plane tickets." Now she just thought she had totally stumped me. She gave me the objection that I could not overcome. They are non-refundable plane tickets and we would lose a lot of money.

My reply was, "That is okay. This is that important."

"Is it that important to go even though we would have to eat the tickets?"

"Yeah, it is that important."

"Okay, then let us do it." And we went to the seminar. Now the seminar itself ended up being life-changing. I am not exaggerating. So many things were life-changing out of that seminar. So many amazing things happened. I learned about a principle called procession, one of Buckminster Fuller's principles, and procession literally shifted the way that I sell.

Procession is bodies in motion affecting bodies in motion. When you take action towards a goal, there are side effects or unexpected things that happen as a result of taking action. And what shifted me as it relates to procession is who I was being in the sales presentation.

What I began to focus on and have focused on ever since then, is when you are delivering your sales presentation, it is not about you. It is all about the prospect. So focus on adding value. Not on your commission, not on what you get out of it, but focus on the value that you are going to add to your client as a result of them being in the presentation with you. That is something that took on a new meaning for me at this seminar. How did I "close" the sale, get my wife to agree to come with me? I was unreasonable!

It is totally unreasonable to say to somebody that has non-refundable plane tickets to just eat the tickets. What is going to happen for you is you are going to be talking to somebody, and they are going to give you an objection, and you are going to be unreasonable. You are going to ask for the sale and let us say you are asking for $300. They say, "I do not have the money."

You are going to say, "Look, this is so important that I want you to go into your closet and find things that you can sell for the $300. That is how important this is."

Or you are going to say to them, "Look, go get a second job until you can come up with the 300 bucks."

Or you are going to say to them, "Look, I know you know somebody in your family that you could borrow that money from. This is that important."

Now this in my opinion is totally unreasonable. But sometimes in life, it is that important. And sometimes you have things going on with your loved ones, your children, your spouse, your parents, where it is important for you to be unreasonable. You need to communicate to them how important it is, whatever it is that you are trying to communicate. So be unreasonable.

The Close

Now what we have been covering here is so important. Think about this, you have set the appointment, you delivered the presentation, and maybe you have been with the prospect for 45 minutes. They truly need what you are offering, and they give an objection. It is the final step before that sale closes, and it is so important that you are effective with this.

These are the tools that I have learned that have made a tremendous difference for me, and they can do the exact same thing for you.

11 Things You Can Do Right Now

7

POIs

The first of the eleven ideas that I want to share is an idea that will probably generate a million dollars in sales for my company and it can possibly generate even more for you! If you are wondering, the answer is YES, you can absolutely model this idea!

I am going to walk you through this step-by-step case history of what I did about 90 days ago. I am going to give you the exact thought process that I had, the questions I asked myself, how I put it into action, and how it is already started creating cash for me. You can do the same thing in your business.

You may remember the POI (Person of Influence) concept where you sell by leveraging networks. Starbucks teamed up with Barnes and Noble to leverage the foot traffic that Barnes and Noble receives. Ask yourself the question, who is a person of influence that has my target market in their network? One valuable exercise that I did three or four months ago is I made a list of all of the POIs that I could think of. I want you to do that same thing. Make a list of all of the POIs that you can think of.

I made a list of all the POIs I could think of, and I finalized it at 132 POIs. Then I stepped back and I thought, okay, I cannot go deep with 132 people. It is too many. How am I going to approach this? What I decided is that I wanted to go deep with four POIs.

I looked at my POIs and I have some amazing people on this list of 132 people. I asked myself, what are my best four opportunities based on synergy, relationship and the size of their lists? The four people I selected were Alex Mandossian, Brian Klemmer, Loral Langemeier and Berny Dohrmann of CEO Space. I then reached out to each of these individuals to let them know of my intention to build a deep relationship with them. I already had a relationship with all of them, but I wanted to go much deeper. Just the other day I teamed up with Loral Langemeier, and we taught an event together.

She was on my list and I e-mailed her, and I said, "Loral, I want to explore ways that we can work together." We got on the phone and we started talking. What we decided to do was to do an event together. So she promoted it to her list and I promoted it to my list. So we doubled our attendance by teaming up and then we cut our expenses in half. That was the first step and shows you how easily it can be done.

Here are your action items. Make a list of the potential POIs for you. Identify the ones where you want to take your relationship deeper. You can start out with four, as I did, because that is a manageable number. Then reach out to those four people and let them know what your intentions are. Schedule a phone appointment or a face-to-face meeting and then see what happens. What I have chosen to do with each of these people is what I call a reciprocal referral relationship, where I am supporting them, referring them, promoting them, and then they are doing the same for me.

● ● ●

Focus on Today

Sometimes I find myself in a place of overwhelm. I might have multiple projects going on, or I might be dealing with things happening in my family or things happening in my business and there is just a lot that is happening. And any time that I find myself in overwhelm, what I do is I just come back to the present moment.

I typically work until about 5:00. So I think in terms of all I need to do is focus on the action items that are right in front of me until 5:00. I do not need to be concerned with tomorrow. I do not need to be concerned with next week or next month. All I need to focus on is peak performing today.

Just part of a recent week for me looked like this: I was in San Francisco with an all-day training on Tuesday and then Tuesday night I flew to Orange County. Then I trained in Orange County on Wednesday with Loral Langemeier. Then I flew back home that night. Then Thursday I was doing my thing at my corporate headquarters in Roseville, had a scripting call that morning, had my Protégé call in the afternoon, and then I was on a plane Friday to Las Vegas for a seminar I was giving. It was a very busy, active, and productive week.

It would have been really easy for me to be in a place of overwhelm. But what I have experienced for myself is I rarely perform at my peak when I am overwhelmed. So I just take it one day at a time and I focus on the present moment. It does not mean the future is not important and I am not going to plan for it, it just means that I am only going to take care of what is right in front of me today.

● ● ●

Focus on Opportunity

Focus on opportunity, not fear, panic or worry. Fear, panic and worry — I am sure that you have realized this — do not manifest money. And although we are in a challenging economic environment, there is amazing opportunity right now.

Recession equals opportunity.

Your brain cannot focus on scarcity and abundance at the same time. Part of the purpose of your subconscious mind is to answer whatever question you ask yourself. So ask yourself this question: Where are my best opportunities right now?

There are so many exciting opportunities with the Internet, with social media, with social networking and even with video. Think about this, right now you can put video up on the web absolutely free. You have so much opportunity in going out and building strategic alliances. When I reached out to Berny Dohrmann of CEO Space, Loral Langemeier, Alex Mandossian and Brian Klemmer, I think one of the reasons why they were really open to working with me in a formal strategic alliance is that they, too, are looking for ways to grow their business right now.

The fact that other people may be in pain right now could be an opportunity of why they would be willing to partner with you. There are lots and lots of tremendous opportunities for you right now. When you get connected to that idea, all of a sudden, the fear, panic and worry go right out the window. You start to feel like; I am so excited I cannot wait to get to work today, because there are so many wonderful opportunities right now.

● ● ●

Optimize Your Business

Optimize your business. This is a concept that I learned from Jay Abraham and my understanding is that Jay Abraham learned it from W. Edwards Deming. If you are not familiar with Deming, you want to Google him and become familiar with Deming's teachings.

Optimizing your business starts with realizing that a chain is as strong as its weakest link. You are going to take a step back from your business and you are going to break your business down into sections. Then you are going to ask yourself the question, how can I optimize this area of my business?

Examine your referral system. My question to you right now is, have you optimized your referral system? If the answer is no, then say, how can I optimize my referral system? For some of you, you need to get a referral system first, and then you could optimize it.

Look at your lead generation. How do you currently generate leads? And then the question is, have you optimized your lead generation? I have multiple lead generation systems, and they work very, very well. And if I ask myself the question, have I optimized lead generation? The answer is absolutely not. This answer forces you to start looking for ways of what you could do to optimize it. Start asking, how can I maximize it and improve it, make it better?

The optimization concept could be applied to any area of your business. If in your business if it involves hiring, have you optimized your hiring system? Have you optimized your sales scripts? As you start going through this, you realize there are so many areas that you can improve. Then start focusing on improvement in those areas.

Out of focusing on those areas you will get better. And then the fear, panic and worry go sailing out the window.

Expand Your Comfort Zone

The number one thing that I found that holds us back from our potential is self esteem. And it is interesting. I know this very well because as a young kid, I worked being a line cook at McDonald's, and I can remember being a line cook at McDonald's as if it was yesterday. One thing I remember when I worked there was they initially trained me on a grill called 4-to-1. The 4-to-1 grill is four patties to one pound. That was the quarter-pounders and back then they had the McDLT. That is the grill I first learned on. Then there is a grill called 10-to-1, and that is ten patties to a pound. On 4-to-1 you'd usually cook one, two or three hamburgers at a time. And because it is a quarter pound it is much thicker than a 10-to-1 patty, so it cooks slower, and you are only cooking one, two, or three at a time typically. On 10-to-1, the patties are much thinner, they cook much faster, and you would typically cook 12 at a time. In some very busy times, you would cook 36 patties at once. And these patties are cooking incredibly quick.

I remember there was a day when I came in for my shift on 4-to-1, and they said, Eric, we need you on 10-to-1 today. And I said, "Well actually, I do not know 10-to-1."

They said, "We do not have anyone else here, so you are on 10-to-1 today." I remember being completely intimidated by that grill. That is where my mindset was, and I can remember that as if it was yesterday. Of course I have come a long way since then, but it is interesting because I have had some circumstances in my life where that old self esteem has showed up again. My experience for myself and in coaching people all over the world is that we get trapped by our comfort zones.

There are opportunities that are available for you right now. They are right there within your grasp. And it is just simply out of your comfort zone. What is been amazing in my experience with all of the things happening in the economy is it is given me this rocket fuel to break through comfort zones. Every once in a while I will get in one of these stretches where I am just out taking massive action. And the economy is creating this massive motivation and I want to open you up to that possibility right now to seek out opportunities that are out of your comfort zone.

It is counterintuitive, because our intuition tells us to stay within our comfort zone. Thoreau said, "Once the mind expands, it will never return to its original size."

Track Your Results Daily

This is something I learned when I worked for the Tony Robbins organization. I learned the importance of tracking. Always remember this, whatever you track; you will see an increase in your results. When I worked for McDonald's, they used to track their inventory every hour. You may have heard me say the joke before, my first job I did so well I made over a hundred thousand. I did not make $100,000, I made 100,000 hamburgers. While, yes it is a joke, I can tell you I honestly made 100,000 hamburgers. On any given shift on the 10-to-1, I would cook 1,000 hamburgers in an eight-hour shift. I worked more than 100 of those shifts. So I literally made over 100,000 hamburgers.

Every hour at McDonald's they print out a report and they know exactly how much of what that they sold. Tracking is one of the big reasons for McDonald's success. So

I want you to think about where do you want to see an increase in your results? And then start tracking it.

I got together with my sales team at the beginning of October. And we had a conversation about new revenue. I shared with them, I said, "Listen team, you get what you focus on, and we are future gazillionaires. The revenues going to come in down the road, but we need revenue now." And so what I told them is, "We are going to start tracking our new revenue, our recurring revenue, and then the revenue generated by my inside sales team. So the revenue that my inside team created, that is one bucket. Then recurring revenue's another bucket and then new revenue is the last bucket. At the end of the month, we will spike in new revenue, because we focused on it.

I am sharing with you exactly what I am doing in my own company. You will want to do the same thing in your business. What areas of your business do you want to see increases in?

Do you want to see increases in referrals? Track it.
You want to see increases in appointments? Track it.
You want to see increases in online leads? Track it.
You want to see an increase in recruits? Track it.
You want to see an increase in team recruits? Track it.
You want to see an increase in average revenue per run appointment? Track it.

Get clear on the results that you want to create, and then track it. You can use a simple Excel spreadsheet to keep track of how you are doing.

● ● ●

Plan Your Day on Paper

Plan your day on paper before the day starts. Even though I teach this information and I consider myself a time management expert, there are times when I struggle with consistently writing down my intentions for the day. And I know how valuable it is. And I know when I do it, I see increases in my results. Yet there are times when I still struggle with that. If I am struggling with it, you may struggle with it as well.

When I do not follow through and plan my day, I do not beat myself up. I acknowledge it, and then I make a decision to get back on track. Life is a series of being on track and then we are off track. And then we are on track, and then we are off track. Because of that, that is exactly why I offer my Silver Protégé Program with a weekly 30-minute call, because it is designed to help sales professionals. If you will just plug in once a week, live or on the recording, just for 30 minutes a week, consistently, it'll help bring you right back on track, get you back in the conversation to stay focused on what is going to help you create results in your business.

Sometimes we know what to do, but we do not always do what we know.

Sometimes it is just simply about taking action.

Collapsing Timeframes

I am in a period in my business right now where I am utilizing this concept and this will help you.

It is an interesting idea.

It is called collapsing timeframes. I picked it up from a guy names Hubert Humphrey. Hubert used to be a top producer for Primerica. Hubert watched A.L. Williams, the owner of Primerica, sell Primerica for millions and millions of dollars. A.L. Williams sold it for so much money that he joined the Forbes list for being one the wealthiest Americans.

Hubert Humphrey watched this, and even though he was making great money as a producer for Primerica. He said, "You know what? I am going to do what A.L. Williams did. I am going to go start my own Primerica and I am going to sell it down the road for millions of dollars and do it just like A.L. Williams."

You know what Hubert did? He did exactly that. He started a company called WMA, World Marketing Alliance. He built it up and several years ago he sold it to Aegon for millions and millions of dollars.

One of Hubert's concepts that I have never forgotten and have implemented at numerous times, including right now as I write this book, is collapsing time frames. It is where you do 90 days worth of work in 30 days.

Let me give you an example of what my day was like over the last, say, 36 hours (I am not suggesting that you work at this level, but it is just something that is happening in my life right now). Yesterday, I taught a seminar with Loral Langemeier.

I was not speaking until the afternoon, but I thought, you know what? I am just going to go down and be in the room. I did not have any expectations. I am just going to be in the room and we'll see what happens. Loral was speaking at 9, and she came down at about 8:30 and the doors were not open yet. Because I just happened to be in the room, we got a chance to have some one-on-one time. Loral decided to rehire me to train her sales team. And that all happened in about a five-minute span in the meeting before the meeting. This is something for you to think about. Arrive at events early and there are often opportunities that will present themselves.

Then Loral started speaking and I went up to my hotel room and I finished up the website for ultimatesellingpowerseminar.com. I got that off to the web person. I am working with my editor on another book, and I made some progress on that. Then it was my turn to speak and I went down and I spoke, and shared information with about 100 people. I then hopped on a plane and flew back home. I had a couple of chapters left in my book and worked on them via audio recordings that I have transcribed. So last night at 11:30 at night, I did one of the two chapters in another book. I have a client on the East Coast that could only meet with me this morning at 6:00 AM, so I scheduled an appointment with him. Then I had a client meeting at 9:00 in the morning, and then at 10:00 this morning I did a conference call for about a hundred people.

That is working at a pretty intense clip. I am not suggesting that you work at that intense of a clip. What I am suggesting is that there may be times in your life to collapse timeframes. If you really get laser focused for short periods of time, you can sprint in your business, and you would be amazed at what you can accomplish.

Complete Your Scripts

Imagine what it would look like if you got three of your most important scripts completed between now and the end of the month. Think about how much more money you could make with those three scripts written out and optimized. They could be presentation scripts, objection handling scripts or closing scripts. Whatever scripts you need most, to increase your effectiveness, are the three scripts that you should get to work on. Again, think of the benefits to you when they are completed and in use. Finishing them this month, would be a great goal.

Focus on Revenue Producing Activities

If you'd like to produce more income now, it is so simple. Sometimes success is very, very simple. It simply comes down to focusing on revenue producing activities. I want you to spend some time before tomorrow morning and think about what can you do on tomorrow to produce revenue? And then focus on that.

Play At A Level 7+

Play at a level 7+ each day.

So here's what that means. In my live seminars, I regularly do the level ten exercise. I get people to think about the level that they have been playing in their life, and I encourage them to make a commitment to step up in the areas that they are not happy with.

You cannot play at a level ten every day. You will burn out.

Consistency is the key.

Consistency is the key.

Consistency is the key.

Having said that, what do many people struggle with? They struggle with consistency.

When you associate with somebody like you are associating with me right now as you read this book, there are certain things that will happen as they will positively influence your life.

Some of their successful traits can rub off on you and you can implement them in your way in your business. One thing that I can honestly tell you, in the 17 years that I have been in commission sales, I have been incredibly consistent every single month. It is one of the things that I have conditioned myself to be.

Tony Robbins talks about conditioning yourself to peak perform. I have conditioned myself to be consistent. So on a scale of one to ten, in terms of effort, energy, and enthusiasm, I challenge myself to play at a level seven or higher every day. My lowest level that I consistently play at is a seven. I do not think people were built to play at a ten every day, but you can consistently play at a seven.

You might reflect right now and say, "Well Eric, I have been playing at a three and I do not think I can get to a seven right now." Okay. If you have been playing at a three, how about your bar starts off at a five and every day moving forward, the lowest level you play at is a five. I am not talking about the weekends and your down time and your recovery time and your relaxation time. I am talking about your business time. When you are focusing on your business, part time or full time, you want to create a standard for yourself, which is your minimum standard.

My standard is seven. I always want to work at level seven or higher and if you will do the same, you will be very successful.

Taking Action

8

Right now, you have a network of people and there are certain doors that you can open for others that will allow that other person just to walk right in, and hopefully book the appointment, or close the sale. A lot of people do this for me, and I also do it for a lot of others.

I want you to think about adding that to your baseline for rest of the year. Look for doors that you can open for other people.

Here is the way I do it:

I will send an e-mail to the person, like in this example the woman's name is Rindi. I send an e-mail to Rindi and then I also included Brad in the e-mail. Then I put in the subject line, the word "Introduction."

In the body of the email I might write something like:

Hi Brad and Rindi,

Brad... (and then I would tell a little bit about Rindi).

Rindi... (I would tell a little bit about Brad).

And then I close with:

I would encourage the two of you to connect.

Out of that, Brad was sharing this victory that he was able to successfully book a speaking engagement with that introduction. This is a time when we as professionals in our various industries need to pull together and look for ways to add value. This is something that is really powerful that you can do for other people.

If you are around me for any length of time, one of the messages you are going to hear me say over and over and over again is to take what you learn from me and look at how you can incorporate the ideas to help you make more sales immediately. I think sometimes when people read a book like this one and you get all this great new knowledge, or you get reminded of things that you have known about in the past, you get very enthusiastic with all the information. However, this does not necessarily mean you are going to instantly see more sales. You need to first apply what you are learning, and then you need to focus on what you want. You get what you focus on. I want you to create a focus on the information in this book and think about how you can implement these ideas today. Think about how to apply at least one of these ideas on your next sales call. I want every single one of you reading this to do your best to take what you learn from what you have read today, and make more sales between now and next week.

I will go to my grave reminding everyone willing to listen that every aspect of the sales process comes down to three ways to increase sales. If you want to increase your sales results, the three ways are: the inner game, the outer game and action.

We have discussed this previously but again, the Inner game is mindset, belief systems, comfort zones, and how you deal with fear of rejection. It is the mental side of selling. There is a mindset to sales greatness. Dr. Moine, my mentor, says selling is 90% psychology. I want you to check in with yourself, if you have any resistance around selling, it is not your fault. There is a stigma to sales in our culture.

That is one of the reasons I remind those in my Protégé Programs about staying in the conversation of sales greatness. By continuing to stay in the conversation with me if you have a resistance to selling, you can make a break through over the next 12 months.

The outer game of sales is your how-to's, your step-by-step, your systems. How do you close? How do you handle objections? How do you book appointments? How do you generate leads? How do you use a database? It is the how-to's of actually generating a sale.

The third component is action. In this chapter, we are focused on taking action. A lot of people do not know this, but action is a skill set. Most people take action and then they immediately look for a result.

Results take as long as they take.

How long is it going to take for you to become a sales champion? I do not know the answer to that. That is why in my teachings, I stress the number one goal is to stay in the conversation. By staying in the conversation, you will get it when you get it, because you never know when you are going to have the breakthrough.

Even at my level I still I still have breakthroughs. Stay in the conversation. Focus on activity, not results.

I remember having a coaching session with one of my clients who was in a sales slump. What did they do? They decreased their activity, which is completely the wrong thing to do when you are in a sales slump. And I told them, look forget about what your results are, take the actions of a sales champion. One thing that you have control over, regardless of what your results are, you have control over action and your mindset. So identify the actions that you need to take tomorrow, and then go out and do it, and give it your best result.

Sometimes you get paid today, and sometimes you do not, but you always get paid.

You will be fairly compensated in due time.

I remember giving a speech in Palm Springs. There were almost 1,000 people in the audience, and based on my average results, I was expecting to produce $10,000 out of that speech. I gave the speech, but the speech did not land. I only did $800 in sales. Based on the actions, I produced $10,000 in value, but it only produced $800 in revenue. And so I said to myself, sometimes you get paid today, and sometimes you do not, but you always get paid.

And what I also said to myself was, the universe owes me $9,200. Sometimes in business, sales just fall into our lap without very much action. Other times we have to work really, really hard for it. If you are going out and putting forth the effort, just know that you will be fairly compensated in due time.

Results take as long as they take.

There is a weight loss reality show called "The Biggest Loser," and while I do not like the title, it is a great show about how people transform their health and their weight loss. One of the interesting things about the show is they do a weigh-in every week. These are people in a secluded environment, working with the best trainers in the world, they are eating the perfect diet, I mean this is like the optimum environment to lose weight. In some cases, somebody would do everything right, they take all the right actions, they get on the scale and they would not have lost any weight. But see, if you consistently take the right actions in this game, "The Biggest Loser," eventually you will lose the weight but from week to week you do not always see the results.

Why I am bringing this up is that this is the number one reason why people do not take more action. In their mind they go, well, it is a waste of time. Using "The Biggest Loser" example, here I ate everything right, worked out right, did it perfectly, and I did not lose any weight, forget this, and they give up. That is a story of people's lives that happens over and over and over again. They give up. In some cases they were right on the verge of a breakthrough.

I have experienced breakthroughs in my life many times. And each time just prior to the breakthrough, I did not realize how I was right on the verge of it.

A story that you may be familiar with is when I was on quarterly probation working for Dante Perano many years ago, I was the bottom producer about to be fired from my job. Then I met Dr. Moine and started learning his techniques. I made my quarterly quota by one sale. So I am 13 months into my sales career and I am the bottom guy. In the 14th month I became the top producer.

Now, I did not become the top producer overnight. During those 13 months, I was developing my great habits. I actually was making the most phone calls out of everybody on the team. I was working on my skills. But it took me 13 months before I had my breakthrough. It was the 14th month when I had the breakthrough and if I had quit prior to my 14th month, my breakthrough would have never happened and my life would undoubtedly be quite different.

If you interviewed me in the 13th month and asked, "Eric, how would you describe your sales skills?"

I would say, "I am the bottom producer and not very good." I did not know that I was days away from a breakthrough to become the top producer in my division, and then seven months later become the top producer in the entire company.

You may be inches away from a breakthrough and you just have got to keep taking action.

Focus on activity, not results.

One of the secrets, if you will, to my successes, is that I take life very much one day at a time. I looked at my calendar today, I looked at my appointments, I looked at my outcomes, I looked at what it is that I need to accomplish and I am not concerned about tomorrow, next week, next month, or next year. And I absolutely plan. The planning is key, but during the business day, I am focusing on the present moment.

When you just narrow it down to the present moment, it allows you to get focused to take the action that you need to take.

Identify the actions that a successful person would take in your industry, on a daily basis.

So let us say you are a real estate agent, here's the question; what do successful real estate agents do?

Let us say you are a coach. What do successful coaches do?

Let us say you are in network marketing. What do successful network marketers do?

And then go and do those things. What habits would a person have that is successful in your industry? What would they believe? What actions would they take? This is one of my all time favorite quotes, "The universe rewards people who take action differently than those who do not."

I was speaking at a conference called SANG and there is this gentleman named Bill Glazer's in the audience. Bill Glazer's business partner is Dan Kennedy. These guys are big deals in the speaking world; they are two of the elite guys out there right now.

I had never met Bill before, but I knew he was in the audience. I went up to him at the end of the day and I said, "Bill I just want to introduce myself to you, and I wanted to let you know that I have a large e-mail list and I would be happy to promote one of your programs if you would like me to."

Bill said, "You know Eric, I do not think I would really be interested in that."

I was like, okay... I mean I kind of felt rejected. Here I am offering him this thing and he is saying "I am not interested in that."

But he says to me, "You were on the panel earlier today right?"

"Yeah, I was on the panel. I was on the panel on how to sell in a new economy."

"I really liked what you had to say. I would like you to be on one of my monthly interviews."

They have a protégé program too called the Gold Protégé Program.

"I would like to interview you and mail out that CD to all of my members. If you are looking for more clients that would really help you. Would that interest you?"

That is something that is going to happen for me this year. It happened because I went up to Bill and asked him if I could do something for him. And he blew me away with that offer. There are offers like that, that are available to you that could more your business forward faster. And all you have to do is take action.

There is a saying that 80-percent of success is showing up. There is one thing that you have the option to do. You have the option to join my Silver Protégé program and participate in every call that I provide this year. It is a 30-minute call, once a week. You can listen to the recording if you cannot make the live call. That is one thing that every one of you has the option to do. The people that show up and stay in the conversation, they get great results.

Here is a powerful affirmation. I am a master of action. The raw belief is, whatever you tell yourself over and over again, you will eventually believe. Tell yourself right now, I am a master of action. Listen to what the little voice in the back of your head tells you, because for some that little voice will go, no you are not, who are you trying to kid? You might be a master of procrastination, but not a master of action. That little voice that talks to us. The law of belief is whatever you tell yourself over and over again, you will eventually believe.

I have themes for myself and one of the themes is, a year of alignment. And another theme, this is a year of massive action. Create a slogan for yourself for the rest of the year, and maybe for you this is the year of massive action. Or maybe this is the year that you get your scripts done. Or maybe this is the year of time management or organization. You can have more than one slogan for the year. This is the year for massive action.

Measure prospecting by played appearances, not base hits. In baseball when you play, you do not get a base hit every time, but you can go up and swing the bat every time. That is called a plate appearance. When you are making your prospecting calls, focus on the action of the prospecting calls. Often times I will make tick marks to keep track of how many prospecting calls I make. What do you think I do when I dial a phone number and I get a busy signal? Do you think I make a tick mark? When I dial a phone number and I get a wrong number, do you think I make a tick mark? When I dial a phone number and I get a voice mail, do you think I make a tick mark? And if you answered yes, yes, and yes, you would be right.

Why would I give myself credit for these things? Because everything counts. And it is important I acknowledge the activity. Now that is just me. You could do it any way that you want, but I make a tick mark every time I pick up that phone when I am tracking my activities.

One of the things I focus on are activity goals. With my own sales team, we track results every day, and one of the things that we track is activity. I want to know, how many meetings did you schedule? How many meetings did you run? In some cases we track dials. I want to know what is the activity and how often is it performed, because when you take the right actions, you get the right results.

That is worth repeating. When you take the right actions you get the right results.

If you are not getting the results you want in your life, take a look at what are the actions.

An extreme example of this is Gilbert Arenas. I am a NBA basketball fan, and even if you are not a fan, you might have heard his name because he was suspended from the NBA. He was the guy that brought the gun to the locker room and the Feds were investigating him. So they suspended him indefinitely. The guy makes $100,000 a game, and they just suspended him. Every game he misses he is losing $100,000. So he takes this action, he brings guns to the locker room and then he makes a joke about it. He compounds a bad action with another bad action.

I can tell you, because I have not always taken the best actions in my life, that when you take bad actions, you get bad results.

Start taking a look at the actions that you are taking in all areas of your life. Your finances. Your relationships. Your health. What time you go to bed. What are your actions there? What do you eat for breakfast? How do you keep your desk organized? How many sales calls do you make a day or a week? The actions that you take are directly related to the results that you are producing. So you make a decision to start taking better action and more action, and your life will improve.

The power of the present moment is at any given moment in time, you can make a decision about how your life is going to be different. We can all have a clean slate. Every day is a brand new day. This is a business book, but really we are talking about your life right now. We are talking about the actions that you are taking in your life, not just your business. What actions can you take right now that will stop hurting you?

One of the things about success is that it is a team sport. I am somebody who is had my share of failures in life. One of the things that I have recognized is to reach out when we need help with problems that are bigger than us. That is one of the reasons why I spoke with a heath expert recently. She has spent her entire working life helping people with their health, and I recognize that it is an area where I need to improve. So I was like okay, I need to acknowledge that and I need to get help in that area.

Something I am not embarrassed to admit, is that last year I went to marriage counseling. Why did I go to marriage counseling? Because I was having a problem that was so big that I could not solve it on my own. Thank God my ego was not so big that I was not willing to accept help. I can honestly tell you that it was one of the best decisions I ever made in my life because my wife and I had reached a point in our relationship where we were not effectively communicating. And I did not know how what to do about it. I did not have the skills. As intelligent as I am around selling, that is an entirely different skill set. And so what did I do? I went out and I found a professional that is an expert at relationships and communicating. That is what they do. They help couples communicate better. And I can honestly tell you that my relationship with my wife has never been better. I recognized that my actions on communication were harming my relationship and did something about it.

You can do something similar. Look at every aspect of your professional and personal life and if there are any problem areas, consider hiring a professional to help you solve them.

Remember this; some problems are so big you cannot solve them on your own. No matter how smart you are.

Focus on completion versus perfection. There is a time for perfection, but there is also a time for completion. For some people, just how their brain works, they get stopped at oh, it is got to be perfect and if it is not perfect, then they are not going to do it. If your brain works like that, know you are not alone, a lot of people think like that. And know that you can work on areas of your life of focusing on completion. In some cases it makes sense to focus on completion versus perfection.

In economics, diminishing returns is also called diminishing marginal returns, or the law of diminishing returns. According to this relationship, in a production system, with fixed and variable inputs, say factory size and labor, beyond some point, each additional unit of variable input yields less and less output. Conversely, producing one more unit of output costs more and more in variable inputs. This concept is often known as the law of increasing relative costs or the law of increasing opportunity cost. Although ostensibly a purely economic concept, diminishing marginal returns also implies a technological relationship. Diminishing marginal returns states that a firm's short-run marginal cost curve will eventually increase. In the modern physical system's view, diminishing returns is a stage and learning curve of development in environmental responses for any individual physical system, beginning with positive marginal returns and leading to a system wide point of diminishing returns when the sign of marginal return reverses.

So what does that all mean? That means that if you consistently work 18 hours a day, that is not your most productive state.

You get to a point in the workday when the more you work, the less productive you are. In theory, we would think, the more I work, the more results I get. But based on the law of diminishing returns, it does not work that way. So it is something for you to think about as you are trying to get better results.

Yes, it is about taking action, and it is more important, not only to be taking action, but taking the right actions.

The Power of the Written Word

Consistently write down the actions that you are going to take. Use a system to do this. I am going to say that again, consistently write down the actions that you are going to take.

One system that I have found that works for me is when I write down my intentions or my to-do's for the day, I take more action. I want you to try that out for yourself, write down your intentions to take more action.

About Eric Lofholm

Eric Lofholm is a Master Sales Trainer who has trained tens of thousands of sales professionals nationwide. He is President and CEO of Eric Lofholm International, Inc., an organization he founded to serve the needs of sales professionals worldwide.

Eric began his career as a top-producing sales representative for 3 different sales organizations. His consistent track record of regularly outperforming his fellow sales reps earned a reputation of success that follows him to this day.

Eric has been trained by the top trainers of his time including: Anthony Robbins and Dr. Donald Moine Ph. D. as well as countless others.

Many of America's top companies hire Eric regularly to train, motivate, and inspire their sales teams. His clients have added millions of dollars in sales to their record after attending Eric's energetic and groundbreaking seminars.

Mentors Magazine, featured Eric in a recent issue. Linda Forsythe, Publisher, said, "I am delighted to bring to you a transcript of my wide-open conversation with Eric Lofholm. Eric is a world-class sales training guru, as you will discover in this interview. As a sales trainer, he has commanded the respect, and in fact has trained salespeople from hundreds of companies including: Century 21, Wells Fargo, Microsoft, Prudential and Toyota just to name a few. Even Anthony Robbins turned to Eric to increase his sales results. Eric trained Tony's trainers over a two year period."

Eric also is an instructor for Quattro University and a Networking University faculty member.

Eric has delivered more than 1,600 public and private presentations throughout the world.

Eric Lofholm International, Inc.
(888) 817-2537

Breinigsville, PA USA
24 May 2010
238551BV00002B/2/P